A Different BATTLE:

Stories of Asian Pacific American Veterans

Edited by

Carina A. del Rosario

with a Historical Essay by

Ken Mochizuki and Carina A. del Rosario

Contemporary Photographs by

Dean Wong

Wing Luke Asian Museum, Seattle   University of Washington Press, Seattle & London

Printed in the United States of America by Graphic Arts Center.

Wing Luke Asian Museum edited, with permission, excerpts of interviews conducted by Densho Japanese American Legacy Project, Filipino American National Historical Society and Seattle Sansei.

Library of Congress Number 99-65748

Carina A. del Rosario is a freelance writer. Her articles have appeared in *The Seattle Times*, the *San Jose Mercury News* and the *International Examiner,* a Seattle newspaper focusing on Asian Pacific Americans.

Ken Mochizuki is the author of the picture books *Baseball Saved Us, Heroes* and *Passage to Freedom: The Sugihara Story.* As a journalist, he has extensively covered the experiences of the Asian Pacific American veteran, particularly those who served in Vietnam.

Dean Wong is a photographer whose work has appeared in *The Seattle Times* and the *International Examiner* as well as Seattle galleries. Seattle's Asian and Pacific Islander communities are his primary subjects.

Founded in 1967, the Wing Luke Asian Museum has documented and presented the history of the Pacific Northwest's different Asian and Pacific Islander communities. Its other publications are: *Divided Destiny: The History of Japanese Americans in Seattle; Reflections of Seattle's Chinese Americans: The First 100 Years; They Painted from Their Hearts: Pioneer Asian American Artists.* The museum is named after Seattle City Councilman Wing Chong Luke, the first Asian Pacific American elected to public office in the Northwest in 1962. Prior to his political career, he served in the military during World War II.

Pictured on cover are
(*background*) Camilo M. "Rammy" Ramirez, U.S. Army Philippine Scouts, 1940 – 1961. Courtesy of Camilo M. "Rammy" Ramirez, 1943.
(*foreground*) James Locke, U.S. Army, 1941-1945
Photo by Dean Wong, 1999.

Pictured on back cover
Andy Cheng is greeted by his family at McChord Air Force Base after returning from the Persian Gulf War on March 21, 1991. Cheng served with the 50th General Hospital Unit in Saudi Arabia. His unit was based out of Fort Lewis, Tacoma, Washington.
Photo by Dean Wong.

Cover and book design by Jesse Doquilo

Table of Contents

Preface

As early as the 1980s, the idea for an Asian Pacific American veterans project had been floating around among members of Seattle's Asian Pacific American community. Ken Mochizuki had published a series of interviews with Vietnam veterans. The Wing Luke Asian Museum sponsored events in Seattle, such as the screening of *Looking Like the Enemy*, a documentary film by Robert Nakamura, and forums featuring veterans or examining war.

In 1998, the idea finally took root when the Wing Luke Asian Museum began research and production of an exhibit to showcase the contributions of Pacific Northwest veterans. The exhibit, *A Different Battle*, opened at the museum in May 1999. Because of the richness of the material collected, the museum decided to produce this book so that more people could be touched by the moving stories of veterans of Asian and Pacific Islander descent.

What do we want people to learn from this? Asian Pacific American veterans and community members puzzled over this question while planning the exhibit and book. We want to acknowledge and honor the thousands of people of Asian and Pacific Islander descent who fought in or with the United States Armed Forces, whose efforts have long been overlooked. We want people to see the faces of Asian Pacific Americans wearing U.S. military uniforms, fighting on the U.S. side.

Beyond this recognition of military participation, however, is the desire to present the reality of war. We want to give people a look at war from the eyes of those who experienced it.

So often, we learn history through the experiences of prominent people. Whether they are presidents or generals, monarchs or religious leaders, history is told from a limited perspective. From these leaders who are quoted in books, newspaper articles and television news, people learn about the ideological, political and economic motivations behind all wars. They learn key events: the start of the war; significant battles; and the end of the war. It is easy to become detached. It is easy to regard war simply as an event, something that just happened.

This objective distance, however, prevents us from seeing war's deep impacts. We overlook how war shapes the lives of those who survive it. All the individuals interviewed for this project share how the wars they fought in changed them — for better or worse. Ten, 30, 40, over 50 years after the fact, they can vividly recall what they went through on the front lines, in the rear or stateside. They can explain how those events tested their abilities, formed their views of life and relationships. Many of them have very painful memories, memories that continue to haunt them after all these years. Still, they want to share so others can learn. Though the veterans each have their own views about the necessity of war, all agree: War is not the adventure and glory usually depicted in films — images they themselves believed when they were young. War is "a hell hole," as World War II veteran Henry Yuen Chin describes it. "It's a lot of pain and a lot of screaming before soldiers die."

By detailing the history and presenting the personal accounts of Asian Pacific American veterans, the people of this project hope that readers consider war's broad impacts on nations, communities, families, and most important, on individuals. Perhaps then, we will work much harder for peace.

Carina A. del Rosario
Project Director and Editor
Seattle, Wash., 1999

Proving Ground

The History of Asian Pacific Americans
in the U.S. Armed Forces

"One time I wore this cap, it says Vietnam Veteran, and I went to the VA hospital. I was standing in the hallway, and I heard two guys talking. One guy looked at me and said, 'I wonder which side he was serving on?'"

—Howard Kim, Vietnam War, U.S. Army[1]

The general public's image of the American GI has been limited. Whether a sailor, pilot, Marine or infantryman, it's a male Caucasian face in that uniform. This picture of the American soldier has been shaped largely by the media. Caucasian stars like Errol Flynn, John Wayne, Tom Cruise and Tom Hanks have starred in Hollywood war movies. Even recent films, where there are some African Americans, Native Americans and Mexican Americans, the only Asian faces are usually those on the side of the enemy.

Filmmakers, however, don't hold the sole responsibility of representing war and the military. Historians and the U.S. military itself have failed to acknowledge the contributions of Asian Pacific American veterans. The U.S. military realizes this. "It is only in recent years that detailed records of this minority's service in the military have been kept," said Lt. Col. F.T. Fowler of the United States Marine Corps. "The history of Asian Pacific American participation in the U.S. Armed Services is very poorly recorded and generally referred to only coincidentally."[2]

For 250 years, Asians and Pacific Islanders have been immigrating to the United States; for almost as long, they have been bearing arms on her behalf. People of Asian and Pacific Islander descent have been fighting in or with the U.S. Armed Forces for at least 187 years. It is important to give them the recognition they are due while also challenging people's misconceptions about who is American. By reading about the contributions of these veterans, the American public may realize how Asian Pacific Americans have shaped U.S. history.

1 Howard Kim, interview with Debbie Abe, November 14, 1998.
2 Lt. Col. F.T. Fowler, United States Marine Corps, "Asian Pacific American Heritage Week." The Research Division of the Defense Equal Opportunity Management Institute (DEOMI), Florida: Patrick Air Force Base, December 1989.

The First Wave:
Immigration and Service
before World War I

Filipinos were the first Asian/Pacific Islanders to settle permanently and form their own communities in North America. Forced into labor aboard Spanish galleons since the 16th century, Filipinos sailed from their native islands to the shores of Mexico and present-day California. By the 18th century, these Filipino sailors began to escape from their Spanish masters and travel across Mexico, settling in Louisiana. Many of these Filipino settlers fought for America during the War of 1812. Pirate Jean Lafitte, operating out of Barataria Bay near the Gulf of Mexico, recruited local Filipinos into his private navy. As many as 400 Filipinos from the Manila Village settlement on Barataria Bay served at some time with Lafitte's force of 3,000. The American government declared Lafitte and his followers criminals. As overwhelming British forces sent the American Army reeling and captured Washington, D.C., during the war, American Gen. Andrew Jackson agreed to grant Lafitte and his followers amnesty if they fought for the Americans during the Battle of New Orleans. This critical battle would determine which country would have control of the Mississippi River. Lafitte arrived in time with his men and the desperately needed ammunition, proving decisive for an American victory against the British. That battle turned the tide of the war.[3]

In 1852, during a time of war and famine in China, a Chinese father in Canton sold his 10-year-old son for $6 to a New England sea captain. During the two-month

Joseph Pierce, circa 1862.

voyage to America, the ship's crew nicknamed the boy "Joe." The family that adopted him in Hartford, Conn., gave him the name Joseph Pierce.

In 1862, Pierce joined the Union Army's 14th Connecticut Regiment to oppose the Confederates in the War between the States. The 14th fought in some of the bloodiest battles of the Civil War, including campaigns at Antietam, Fredericksburg, Chancellorsville and Gettysburg. By the war's end in 1865, when Pierce was discharged from the Army as a corporal, the 14th had lost more men than any other Connecticut regiment.[4]

Men of Asian/Pacific Islander descent also fought with U.S. forces during the Spanish-American War, which started in 1898 with the sinking of the *USS Maine*. Seven Issei (first generation Japanese immigrants in America) and one Chinese American were reported to have been among the 253 U.S. Navy crew members killed when the *USS Maine* exploded and sunk in Havana Harbor, Cuba.[5]

The "American-Born Chinese Brigade" was formed in Oregon that same year. Seid Back, Jr., a Chinese American rejected by the U.S. Army due to poor eyesight, formed the brigade with the assistance of the Oregon National Guard during the war. As a captain within the brigade, Back led mostly teenagers in drills and parades. This is the first known military organization for American-born Chinese within the United States.[6]

U.S. land and sea forces fought Spanish forces on territory controlled by Spain, including Puerto Rico and the Philippines. Filipinos fought alongside the U.S. Army to liberate their country from the Spanish. After the 10-month war ended with Spain's defeat, the 1898 Treaty of Paris made the Philippines a territory of the United States. American President William McKinley declared the Philippines "unfit for self-government" and that the United States had no choice but "to take them all, and educate the Filipinos, and uplift and civilize and

---

3 Marina Espina, interview with Ken Mochizuki, Jan. 6, 1999. While a librarian at the University of New Orleans during the 1970s, Espina uncovered the history of early Filipino settlers and interviewed their descendants.
4 John M. Archer, "An Oriental Yankee Soldier," *Civil War Times Illustrated*, September/October 1994.
5 Directorate of Research, Defense Equal Opportunity Management Institute (DEOMI), "Asian Pacific American Heritage Week," Florida: Patrick Air Force Base, Sept. 1998, p. 8.
6 Wing Luke Asian Museum archival collection, Seattle, WA., 1999.
7 *Allies and Enemies: The Dilemma of Asian Americans during World War II*, a Resource Book by The Museum of Chinese in America, New York, 1996, p. 7.

Christianize them."[7] Instead of being granted the independence that Filipinos thought they fought for, the United States established military rule over the Philippines. Feeling betrayed, the same Filipino soldiers who fought alongside U.S. forces during the Spanish-American War turned against their new rulers. Filipinos, led by Gen. Emilio Aguinaldo, battled U.S. soldiers and Marines in what became known as the Philippine Insurrection, 1899-1901. The Insurrection claimed the lives of 4,165 Americans. Over 200,000 Filipinos died, including civilians and 20,000 Filipino fighters, derogatorily called "goo-goos" by the American forces.[8]

To help combat the Insurrection, the U.S. Army formed the 1st Company of Macabebe Scouts with Filipino civilians. These men, from the Macabebe Pampanga region of the Philippines, were historical enemies of the Tagalog-speaking Filipinos who made up the majority of the rebels fighting the U.S. Filipino American historians often cite that the U.S. Army exploited this indigenous hostility the same way that it did in recruiting Native American scouts to fight against other Indian nations in America.[9]

In 1901, Congress authorized the President of the United States to enlist 12,000 native Filipinos into military units called the Philippine Scouts. The U.S. Army made the Scouts an integral part of the Army, with the Macabebe soldiers forming the nucleus. of the Philippine Scouts.[10] From its inception to the beginning of World War II, the Scouts were used mainly to fight against Filipino rebels still resisting U.S. occupation. Much of the resistance came from the Moros tribe in the southern Philippine islands of Mindanao, Samar and Jolo.

That same year, President McKinley also signed General Order No. 40, permitting the U.S. Navy to recruit up to 500 Filipinos from the Philippines to enlist in the Naval Insular Force, a division that allowed Filipino nationals to serve on U.S. military installations in the Philippines. U.S. Navy records indicate that 500 Filipinos joined that year. This initial group of recruits could enlist into Navy duties, or "ratings," that included coxswain, seaman, steward, machinist, coaler and fireman. However, most were assigned and restricted to being stewards, serving food and cleaning officers' quarters.[11] Recruitment of Filipino nationals into the U.S. Navy steadily increased.

A Filipino scout and sailor were the first Asian/Pacific Islanders to receive the highest honor bestowed on a member of the U.S. Armed Forces for bravery: the Congressional Medal of Honor. Pvt. Jose B. Nisperos, of the 34th Company of the Philippine Scouts, was an interpreter for a detachment of U.S. sailors who landed at Lapurap, Balsilan Island, to track down an outlaw chieftain. When the detachment was unexpectedly attacked by a group of Moros on Sept. 24, 1911, the commanding officer was mortally wounded by a poisoned spear. The Moros also wounded Nisperos with spears and shot off his left arm above the elbow. Nisperos fell to the ground, shoved the stump of his severed arm into the ground to stop the bleeding, and continued firing his rifle with one hand. His actions held off the enemy until reinforcements arrived. Nisperos received his medal at a ceremony in Manila two years later.[12]

On Jan. 21, 1915, a boiler exploded aboard the USS San Diego. The explosion drove Fireman 2nd Class Telesforo Trinidad out of the boiler room, but he returned at once to rescue an injured shipmate, Fireman 2nd Class R.E. Daly. Trinidad suffered burns about his face as another boiler exploded; however, he continued to carry Daly out and also assisted in the rescue of another injured seaman.[13]

On the American mainland, Chinese began immigrating to the U.S. beginning in the mid-19th century. Rapidly expanding American industries, particularly the railroads, created a high demand for laborers. Workers from China filled this need until 1882, when Congress passed the Chinese Exclusion Act to prevent more Chinese laborers from entering the U.S. Japanese came in droves to work in America until the "Gentleman's Agreement" in 1907 between the U.S. and Japan limited the number of Japanese permitted to immigrate to America. Immigrants from the Philippines, Korea and India filled the labor void created by the exclusion of Chinese and Japanese. In 1917, Congress created the Asian Barred Zone, which limited immigration by all Asians except for Filipinos and natives of Guam since their countries were territories of the United States. A 1924 immigration bill signed by President Calvin Coolidge ended all immigration from Japan.[14]

8 Fred Cordova, *Filipinos: Forgotten Asian Americans, A Pictorial Essay* 1763-1963, Seattle; Dubuque, Iowa: Kendall/Hunt Publishing Co., 1983
9 Fred Cordova, Filipino American National Historical Society (FANHS), interview with Ken Mochizuki, Dec. 16, 1998.
10 Ibid.
11 Flores, "A Historical Account of the Filipino American Experience in the United States Navy," pp. 9-10
12 *The Congressional Medal of Honor: the Names, the Deeds,* Forest Ranch, California: Sharp & Dunnigan Publishers, 1984, p. 599; FANHS archival document, manuscript titled "Pioneer Filipino to Receive the Medal of Honor."
13 *The Congressional Medal of Honor: The Names, the Deeds,* p. 547.
14 *Allies and Enemies: The Dilemma of Asian Americans during World War II,* p. 7; "Japanese Americans in America's Wars: A Chronology," Los Angeles: Japanese American National Museum, 1999, p. 1.

Segregated Units for People of Color

Camilo M. "Rammy" Ramirez served with the Philippine Army and the US Army Philippine Scouts. Escaping from a Japanese POW camp during World War II, Ramirez found his way to the United States serving a total of 22 years in the military and 28 years with the VA hospital. 1943. —Courtesy of Camilo M. "Rammy" Ramirez.

Asian immigrants lived in different parts of the U.S., working on railroads, in canneries, farms, restaurants and hotels. Though faced with job and housing discrimination as well as citizenship limitations, they reported for duty when America joined the First World War in Europe. Documentation of Asian Pacific American participation in World War I remains sparse, and often only by searching through family histories can a World War I veteran be identified.[15] Members of the Philippine Scouts were known to have fought in World War I.[16] An all-Japanese Company D, 1st Hawaiian Regiment of Infantry was formed in Hawaii, but never saw combat.[17]

The most noted Asian Pacific American World War I veteran was Tokutaro "Tokie" Nishimura Slocum. He immigrated to the United States at age 10 and was among the first Japanese settlers in the North Dakota plains. Adopted by the Slocum family of Minot, N.D., he attended the University of Minnesota and, while a student at Columbia University law school, joined and fought with the 328th Infantry in France. While in combat, Slocum experienced poisonous gas attacks, which caused lifelong medical problems. Slocum attained the rank of sergeant major, becoming the highest-ranking Asian Pacific American in the U.S. Army up to that time. Because he was a war veteran, he was allowed to become a naturalized U.S. citizen

Issei war veterans became ineligible for naturalization because of the 1925 U.S. Supreme Court decision in *Toyota vs. U.S.* Largely through Slocum's one-man crusade and lobbying efforts, Congress passed the Nye-Lea Bill in 1935, granting naturalization rights to 500 World War I veterans of Asian descent.[18]

Between World War I and World War II, the number of Filipino nationals in the U.S. Navy remained constant at approximately 4,000. By 1935, the ratification of the Tydings-McDuffie Act, also known as the Philippines Independence Act, granted independence to the Philippines in 10 years. The Act

15 Jimmie Toy, interview with Ron Chew, Nov. 25, 1998; Raymond Lew, interview with Carina A. del Rosario, Feb. 3, 1999; Henry Yun Chin, interview with Pei Pei Sung, Feb. 1, 1999.
16 DEOMI, p. 16.
17 Japanese American National Museum (JANH), *Japanese American History: An A to Z Reference From 1868 to the Present*, New York: Facts on File, Inc., 1993, p. 352.
18 Ibid., p. 312.

also affected every Filipino in the Philippines and in the United States by stripping them of their status as "nationals," which had been in effect since the end of the Spanish-American War. All Filipinos became "aliens," barring them from immigrating to the U.S. and from becoming U.S. citizens. The only way Filipinos could now become U.S. citizens was by serving in the U.S. Army (the Philippine Scouts) or the U.S. Navy. In the Navy, Filipinos could become citizens after serving a required number of "hitches" (three years equaled a hitch). Usually, three hitches were required. However, the U.S. Navy often changed the number of hitches that had to be served.[19]

World War II:
Surmounting Eligibility Requirements

Prior to U.S. involvement in World War II, Japan had already conquered and controlled much of northern China and Korea. After the attack at Pearl Harbor, Japan immediately attacked and defeated American and Filipino forces defending the Philippines. When the United States declared war against Japan, Chinese, Koreans and Filipinos in America were eager to support the U.S. war effort. Still, because of discriminatory laws, they were not readily accepted in the Armed Forces. For instance, the U.S. Alien Registration Act of 1940 classified Korean immigrants as subjects of Japan and thus, "enemy aliens." The Korean community, however, strove to distinguish itself from any affiliation with the country of Japan. In Los Angeles, 109 Koreans – one-fifth of the city's Korean population – joined the California National Guard and were organized into the Manghokun, or "Tiger Brigade." During December 1943, the U.S. Armed Forces issued an order exempting Koreans from enemy alien status, opening all of the armed services to Korean immigrants. With their knowledge of the Japanese language, Korean Americans proved valuable as interpreters for American forces.[20]

As the U.S. war effort surged and World War II raged in Europe and Asia, the Chinese in America now found new work opportunities previously denied to them. Hundreds of Chinese American men and women found employment in America's defense industries, often in technical and scientific positions offering good wages. The U.S. Navy waived its citizenship requirements and recruited 500 immigrant Chinese as apprentice seamen immediately after the attack on Pearl Harbor. Of the 59,803 Chinese adult males in the U.S. in 1941, over 20 percent were drafted or enlisted in the U.S. Army. Smaller numbers served in the Navy and Air Force. Two hundred fourteen Chinese Americans died in the war.[21]

The 14th Air Service Group of 14th Air Force (the Flying Tigers) was composed entirely of Chinese Americans. More units of the 14th were created as hundreds of Chinese Americans, who could speak Chinese and had aviation-related technical skills, volunteered to serve in China. The 14th, a front-line unit of mechanics who performed aircraft maintenance duties and traveled with the aircraft they serviced, operated in the China-Burma-India Theater in early 1944. Their skills proved critical to the Asian-based air war against Japan – and often made them targets to be bombed and strafed by enemy planes.

As Japanese forces continued their attack on the Philippines in early 1942, an American force of 82,000 Filipino and American soldiers held off the Japanese at the Bataan Peninsula for three months, buying valuable time for U.S. and Allied forces to mobilize for war in the Pacific. Four-fifths of that American force were Filipinos in American uniforms.[22] Among the defenders of Bataan were 12,000 Philippine Scouts under the command of 685 American officers.[23] During the battle of Bataan, another Philippine Scout was awarded the Congressional Medal of Honor.

On Jan. 16, 1942, Sgt. Jose Cabalfin Calugas, Sr., performed his usual duties as a mess sergeant for Battery B of the 88th Field Artillery. While fetching water from a creek, he noticed that American artillery stopped firing as

19 Dorothy and Fred Cordova, FAHNS, interview with Ken Mochizuki, Dec. 16, 1998.
20 Ronald Takaki, *Strangers From a Different Shore: A History of Asian Americans*, New York: Little, Brown and Company, 1989, p. 384.
21 DEOMI, "Asian Pacific American Heritage Week," p. 10.
22 Cordova, *Filipinos: Forgotten Asian Americans*, p. 217.
23 Mark Coltey, "Bravery of local war hero is remembered by many," *Northwest Asian Weekly*, Nov. 8-14, 1997.

Drafted into the US Army Air Force from Seattle in 1942, Horace Loo served with the 8th Air Force in England during WW II. Loo was the radio operator of a B-24 bomber named the "Stinky," and flew 34 missions over France and Germany.
—Courtesy of Mildred Loo and Ron King.

Japanese artillery continued to pound the front lines. Calugas gathered 16 men together and, without orders, led the men across 1,000 yards of ground being heavily shelled. A Japanese plane strafed Calugas' party, hitting two. All retreated except for Calugas and a Philippine Army lieutenant. Calugas and the officer made their way to an American battery, where they found the artillery crew all dead except for two wounded Filipino officers. The four of them repaired the artillery piece and Calugas, the only one not wounded, operated the gun. He single-handedly fired over 70 rounds and stayed with the gun to cover his comrades' retreat, even though his position was bombarded heavily by Japanese artillery. Calugas later survived the Bataan Death March and spent two years in a prisoner-of-war (POW) camp.[24]

Survivors of the march and POW camp attest to the conditions that they had to endure. "While on the road, most everyone complained that they wanted water," said Rosendo Luna, Sr., who served with the U.S. Army's Philippine Scouts. "They would want to go in the well or ditches or the wallow place where the carabou drank. You drag them as long as they could walk. It's very hard in the camps. You have a faucet but you don't have any water. The water we had for taking baths was from the drainage which came from the kitchen because that's the only water you could have. Then the water that you could use in the kitchen, you have to go two miles away from the concentration camp."[25] Because of poor water and food supply, Luna said many prisoners succumbed to illness such as diarrhea, dysentery and malaria. His father died at age 57 in one of the POW camps.

In early 1942, President Franklin Roosevelt authorized draft laws to be changed to include Filipino Americans, who were previously barred from service because of citizenship requirements. On Feb. 19, 1942, Secretary of War Henry L. Stimson announced formation of the 1st Filipino Infantry Regiment: "This new

First and Second Filipino American Regiments pictured at Camp Beale, Calif., Circa 1942. —Courtesy of Lorenzo Umel Pimentel.

24 *The Congressional Medal of Honor: the Names, the Deeds,* p. 277.
25 Rosendo Luna, Sr., interview with Ferdinand de Leon, Dec. 5, 1998.

unit is formed in recognition of the intense loyalty and patriotism of those Filipinos who are now residing in the United States. It provides for them a means of serving in the armed forces of the United States, and the eventual opportunity of fighting on the soil of their homeland."[26] In California, 16,000 – 40 percent of the state's Filipino population – registered for the draft after Stimson's announcement.[27] The 1st Filipino Infantry was activated at Camp San Luis Obispo, Calif. Ironically, this was the site of another seminal event in Filipino American history: As members of a Spanish landing party in 1587, the first Filipinos to set foot on continental North America did so at San Luis Obispo.[28]

With the subsequent formation of the 2nd Filipino Infantry Regiment, the two units combined totaled over 7,000 men. Many of their missions included pre-invasion intelligence work and sabotage after they landed by submarine or parachuted behind enemy lines. The regiments fought in campaigns to capture the islands of Leyte, Samar, and the recapture of the entire Philippines.[29]

Out of the two regiments emerged the 1st Reconnaissance Battalion. Trained in jungle warfare in Australia and New Guinea, the battalion landed by U.S. submarines at locations throughout the Philippine islands. Because they were able to blend in with the local population, they contacted Filipino guerrilla groups and relayed intelligence information to Gen. Douglas MacArthur's headquarters in Brisbane, Australia. Cpl. Dominador F. Gobaleza recounted his experience with the 1st Reconnaissance Battalion: "It was early in 1943 when we began training at the Milton Court, Brisbane, as commandos. While on training, we were asked what dialects [we] can speak fluently, and what place in the Philippines we would prefer to land. These made us much more interested, for once again we will see our beloved land, expecting, of course, the responsibilities we have on hand. The constant question, 'What is now happening to my brother and sister back in our country?' haunted me."[30] American commanders credited the Filipino battalion and regiments with accelerating the recapture of the Philippine Islands.[31]

Samoans joining the United States Marine Corps, 1942.
—Official Marine Corps photo #54702

U.S. Department of Defense records show that Pacific Islanders also participated in the war in the Pacific. The U.S. Navy established itself in Samoa, using the harbor of Pago Pago as a strategic port. U.S. Armed Forces formed the Samoan Marines to defend the islands against a possible Japanese attack. Samoans, Fijians and the native Chamorros of Guam were allowed to enlist in the U.S. Navy and Marine Corps. Their positions included infantrymen, guides, translators and coast watchers.[32]

26 Takaki, *Strangers From a Different Shore*, p. 359.
27 Ibid.
28 Fred Cordova, interview with Mochizuki, Dec. 16, 1998.
29 Mike Markrich, "First Fil," *Transpacific*, Vol. 6 No. 5, September/October 1991, p. 53.
30 Dominador F. Gobaleza, personal testimony, FANHS archival document.
31 Takaki, *Strangers From a Different Shore*, p. 360; Cordova, *Filipinos: Forgotten Asian Americans*, p. 218.
32 DEOMI, "Asian Pacific Heritage Week," p. 12.

Japanese Americans:
From 'Enemy Aliens' to Heroes

While World War II opened up new opportunities for Americans of Asian and Pacific Islander descent, the same could not be said for those of Japanese descent, who lost rights as citizens during the war. After the attack on Pearl Harbor, American politicians and the press circulated unsubstantiated stories — ultimately proven false — about Japanese Americans in Hawaii and the U.S. West Coast. The rumors claimed that Japanese Americans aided the Japanese military before the attack on Pearl Harbor, and would do so again for an impending invasion on the U.S. mainland. By Jan. 19, 1942, any soldier of Japanese ancestry in the U.S. Army was classified "4-C" – "enemy alien." They were disarmed and assigned to menial labor.[33] As hysteria against those of Japanese ancestry peaked, President Franklin Roosevelt signed Executive Order 9066 on Feb. 19, 1942. The order, citing "military necessity," authorized the U.S. Army to remove forcibly all of Japanese ancestry away from the West Coast, expelling 110,000 of them to 10 major concentration camps throughout the United States. Two-thirds of those expelled were born in the United States – American citizens.[34]

No similar mass removal of Japanese Americans took place in Hawaii, where, in fact, Nisei (second generation Japanese Americans) persisted in serving their country. Two thousand Nisei in the U.S. Army were stationed in Hawaii on Dec. 7, 1941. During the Japanese attack on the U.S. naval fleet at Pearl Harbor, Nisei soldiers helped defend against attacking enemy planes.[35] Three days later, the Army authorized formation of the Hawaii Territorial Guard, made up mostly of Nisei Reserve Officers' Training Corps (ROTC) cadets and volunteers from Honolulu high schools, to guard shorelines and vital civilian installations.[36] During February 1942, Gen. Delos Emmons, military governor of Hawaii, formed 169 University of Hawaii students into the Varsity Victory Volunteers (VVV). Attached to the 34th Combat Engineers Regiment, the VVV built roads and fences, strung barbed wire and maintained military buildings.[37]

By June 1942, the Army transferred all Nisei soldiers, except for members of the 1399th Engineering Construction Battalion, out of Hawaii. About 1,400 Nisei Hawaiians were sent to Camp McCoy, Wisc., to begin training as the all-Japanese American 100th Infantry Battalion. The 100th would be the test case, the experiment to determine the loyalty and performance of the Japanese American soldier.[38]

The 100th landed at Salerno, Italy in September 1943. For the next nine months, the 100th engaged in some of the fiercest battles against the German Army in Italy, including battles at Salerno, the Volturno River crossings, Cassino, and the final push from the Anzio beachhead. During this period, members of the 100th were awarded over 1,000 Purple Hearts and became known as the "Purple Heart Battalion."[39] By June 1944, the 100th had fought its way to Rome, and was the closest American unit in position to liberate the city. However, the 100th was ordered to halt while other units were allowed to enter the city first and be welcomed as heroes by masses of cheering civilians.[40]

During January 1943, the Army issued a call for 1,500 Nisei volunteers. In response, 9,507 volunteered.[41] The following month, President Roosevelt officially allowed Japanese Americans back into the U.S. Armed Forces when he wrote to Secretary of War Stimson: "Americanism is not, and never was, a matter of race or ancestry. Every loyal American citizen should be given the opportunity to serve this country."[42] Given the presidential go-ahead, the Army activated the all-Japanese American 442nd Regimental Combat Team (RCT). Training at Camp Shelby, Miss., this regiment was composed of 3,000 men from Hawaii and 1,500 from the mainland – many who volunteered or were drafted out of U.S. concentration camps where their families were surrounded by barbed wire fences and guardhouses with machine guns. More than 300 volunteered from southern Idaho's Minidoka camp, where most of the Japanese Americans from the Pacific Northwest were incarcerated. That number represented the highest number of volunteers from any internment camp.[43] Initially, all officers in the 442nd were Caucasian.[44]

33 Chang, *I Can Never Forget*, p. 97.
34 Takaki, *Strangers From a Different Shore*, p. 379-392.
35 Ibid., p. 384.
36 DEOMI, "Asian-Pacific American Heritage Month 1999," pp. 16-17; JANM, "Japanese Americans in America's Wars," p. 1.
37 DEOMI, "Asian Pacific Heritage Month 1999," p. 17.
38 Chang, *I Can Never Forget*, p. 100; DEOMI, "Asian-Pacific Heritage Month 1999," p. 17.
39 DEOMI, "Asian Pacific American Heritage Week," p. 13; Chang, *I Can Never Forget*, p. 136.
40 Chang, *I Can Never Forget*, p. 143.
41 Takaki, *Strangers From a Different Shore*, p. 385.
42 Ibid., p. 397.
43 David Takami, *Divided Destiny, a History of Japanese Americans in Seattle*, Seattle, Washington: Wing Luke Asian Museum/University of Washington Press, 1998, p. 69.
44 DEOMI, "Asian Pacific American Heritage Week," p. 12.

442nd Regimental Combat Team volunteers from internment Camp Minidoka, Idaho, 1942.
—Courtesy of Wing Luke Asian Museum collections.

MINIDOKA / IDAHO
1942
VOLUNTEERS FOR ARMY

The 442nd landed at Naples, Italy, and merged with the 100th at the port city of Civitavecchia, north of Rome, in June 1944. The 442nd went on to fight in seven major campaigns until the end of the war. In Italy, they captured Livorno and pushed the German Army north of the Arno River. The 442nd suffered 1,272 casualties – more than a fourth of the regiment that was fighting in Italy.[45]

Gen. Mark W. Clark, commanding officer of the 5th Army and commander of the 442nd's Italian campaigns, said: "These are some of the best goddam fighters in the U.S. Army. If you have more, send them over."[46] Soldiers of the 442nd had a more pragmatic view of their performance in combat. Bill Kunitsugu of Seattle said, "We were not supermen, but dedicated soldiers [fighting] to prove our loyalty."[47]

Sent to the Vosges Mountains in northeastern France in October, the 442nd liberated the French towns of Bruyeres and Biffontaine after bitter, house-to-house fighting. After four days of rest, the 442nd was ordered to rescue 211 survivors of the Texas 141st Regiment, 36th Division, who had been surrounded for a week and faced imminent annihilation. In what became known as the rescue of the "Lost Battalion," the 442nd engaged in its fiercest and bloodiest battle: four days of charging uphill through dense forests and fighting a dug-in enemy. After the 442nd reached the Lost Battalion, it suffered over 200 dead and 600 wounded.[48]

"Every morning was when we attacked," Frank Matsuda recalled of the fight to save the Lost Battalion. "That's when everybody got up, started going from tree to tree, moving forward. Then these three machine guns just opened up on U.S. Guys were dropping like flies. This guy Blondie from Hawaii…was shot and it killed him and hit the sergeant…He was groaning, so I went over there and I couldn't do anything…I hollered for a medic but he was too busy doing everybody else 'cause they were getting killed left and right. And so I was fairly close to his head there and I couldn't do much. And he was crying for his mother…"[49]

During March 1945, the 522nd Field Artillery Battalion was detached from the 442nd to join the final Allied push into Germany. The 522nd was among the first to reach the Nazi Dachau concentration camp and liberate its prisoners. The Nisei soldiers witnessed firsthand the horrors of the Nazi death camps, and,

to this day, the inmates saved by them have not forgotten their Japanese American rescuers. "I was 18 years old, 76 pounds at the time, barely alive," said Josef Erbs, a Romanian-born inmate at Dachau. "He picked me up from the ground, inside the camp. His uniform had an emblem – blue, with a white hand and white torch. He was a young Asian man with the American Army. Never before had I seen an Asian man or a black man…."[50]

In April 1945, the 442nd returned to Italy; its mission was to assault the Gothic Line, a seemingly impregnable series of German fortifications in the Apennine mountains of northern Italy. With a frontal assault impossible, the 442nd hoped for a surprise attack by climbing the nearly vertical slopes of Mount Nebione in pre-dawn darkness. After silently climbing for hours, the 442nd attacked and captured two key mountaintop outposts in 32 minutes, causing the eventual collapse of the remaining enemy positions. The 442nd accomplished what repeated Allied assaults could not do for six months.[51]

By the war's end, the 100th and 442nd combined suffered 9,486 casualties, including 650 killed in action. Among the 18,143 individual decorations awarded to the regiment included 9,486 Purple Hearts, 52 Distinguished Service Crosses, and one Congressional Medal of Honor, awarded posthumously to PFC Sadao Munemori.[52]

During the campaign to take the Gothic Line near Seravezza, Italy, Apr. 5, 1945, Pvt. Munemori was pinned down by a strong mountain defense. He assumed command of his squad after its regular leader had been wounded. Munemori led his men through a minefield until they were pinned down by heavy machine gunfire. By himself, Munemori advanced through direct fire and knocked out two German machine guns positions with grenades. Withdrawing under "murderous fire and showers of grenades," he took cover in a crater occupied by two of his men. When an unexploded German grenade bounced off Munemori's helmet and rolled toward his comrades, Munemori dived on the grenade, smothering the blast with his body.[53]

45 Takaki, *Strangers From a Different Shore*, p. 401.
46 Chester Tanaka, *Go For Broke: A Pictorial History of the 100/442nd Regimental Combat Team*, Richmond, California: Go For Broke, Inc., 1982, book jacket quote.
47 Bill Kunitsugu, unpublished autobiography, Seattle, WA, 1998, p. 4.
48 DEOMI, "Asian Pacific American Heritage Week," p. 14.
49 Frank Matsuda, interview with Ken Mochizuki, Jan. 15, 1999.
50 Chang, *I Can Never Forget*, p. 168.
51 Tanaka, *Go For Broke*, pp. 120-125; DEOMI, "Asian Pacific American Heritage Week," p. 14.
52 DEOMI, "Asian Pacific American Heritage Week," p. 15.
53 Tanaka, *Go For Broke*, p. 123; *The Congressional Medal of Honor: the Names, the Deeds*, p. 404.

In 1950 Nisei Veterans Committee raised a memorial in Lake View Cemetery to pay tribute to local Americans of Japanese ancestry who died during military service. By 1999, 64 names have been inscribed.
—Courtesy of the Nisei Veterans Committee, circa 1950.

Military historians believe that the 442nd was the most decorated unit in United States military history.[54] In 1946, President Harry S. Truman presented the Seventh Presidential Unit Citation to the 100th/442nd , stating, "...you fought not only the enemy, you fought prejudice — and you won."[55]

During the course of World War II, more Japanese Americans volunteered or were drafted into the Army to replace soldiers in the 100th or 442nd, or to serve in other units, bringing the total of Japanese American soldiers to 33,000. They also made up the majority of the 1399th Engineer Construction Battalion in Hawaii, and played a key role in the Military Intelligence Service (MIS).[56] In addition to those in the regular Army, an estimated 330 Nisei women were on active duty as members of the Women's Army Corps (WACs) by 1944. Forty-seven Nisei WACs served with the MIS. As translators, they either served in the states or were stationed in postwar Tokyo.[57] Their male counterparts served with the military forces of Australia, China, Britain and New Zealand. After the war, the MIS served with U.S. forces during the occupation of Japan.[58]

When soldiers of Japanese descent were being allowed back into the Armed Forces after the start of World War II, those proficient in the Japanese language were singled out and sent to the Presidio of San Francisco, and later to Camp Savage and Fort Snelling in Minnesota.[59] Studying the Japanese language intensively, some 6,000 of these soldiers either stayed in the states or were shipped overseas to join the war in the Pacific. Members of the MIS served as battlefield interpreters, codebreakers, translators of captured Japanese documents and interrogators of Japanese prisoners. They also often persuaded Japanese soldiers to surrender.

Those on the front lines were often accompanied by a Caucasian GI, serving as a bodyguard to protect the MIS member from harm if he was mistaken for the enemy. MIS soldiers first participated in the invasion of Guadalcanal and defense of the Aleutian Islands. The MIS contributed to the American victory at the Battle of Midway by intercepting and translating enemy messages. Because MIS members were able to translate the Japanese Navy's master plans for defending the Philippines and the Marianas, American forces annihilated the Japanese Imperial Navy in the Philippine Sea. This paved the way for Gen. Douglas MacArthur's return to the Philippines and the U.S. forces' recapture of the Marianas. And in what Gen. MacArthur described as one of the most significant actions of the war in the Pacific, MIS members intercepted and translated enemy messages that led to the ambush and destruction of aircraft carrying Japanese Navy Commander-in-Chief Isoroku Yamamoto, the architect of the attack on Pearl Harbor. Gen. Charles Willoughby, chief of intelligence in the Pacific, said, "The Nisei shortened the Pacific War by two years and saved possibly a million American lives and saved possibly billions of dollars."[60]

54 Takaki, *Strangers From a Different Shore*, p. 402; DEOMI, "Asian-Pacific Heritage Month 1999," cover page.
55 Tanaka, *Go For Broke*, p. 171.
56 Military Intelligence Service Northwest Association (MIS Northwest Association), *Military Intelligence Service National Reunion: Commemorating the 50th Anniversary of the End of World War II*, Seattle, Wash., 1995, p. 35.
57 MIS Northwest Association, *Unsung Heroes: The Military Intelligence Service, Past, Present, Future*, Seattle, Washington, 1996, p. 5.; MIS Northwest Association, *Military Intelligence Service National Reunion*, pp. 35-36.
58 Takaki, *Strangers From a Different Shore*, p. 400; MIS Northwest Association, *Military Intelligence Service National Reunion*, pp. 34-37.
59 Ibid., pp. 33-34.
60 MIS Northwest Association, *Military Intelligence Service National Reunion*, p. 36.

Members gather outside of the American Legion Cathay Post #186 in 1947.
—Courtesy of the American Legion Cathay Post #186, Seattle, Wash.

Racism:

A Constant Battle

While training on American bases during World War II, Asian Pacific American men and women often had to endure hostile and discriminatory treatment off base in nearby local towns. Soldiers of the 1st Filipino Infantry were unwelcome in Marysville, Calif. Asian Pacific American soldiers training in the South found themselves caught in between a color barrier. "I had to go to the bathroom," recalled 442nd veteran Kim Muromoto, "'Colored' and 'White.' Now which one [was] I supposed to go into? There was one Caucasian GI. I think he was kind of puzzled that I was standing there looking to see which one, so he told me: 'You go into the 'White.'"[61]

61 Kim Muromoto, interview with Ken Mochizuki, Jan. 19, 1999.

Even after World War II, when Asian/Pacific Islanders had proven themselves in combat, they were still not fully perceived as Americans. The most often quoted story comes from Daniel Inouye, an officer with the 442nd who would later become a longtime U.S. Senator from Hawaii. Hoping to get a haircut in San Francisco, Inouye walked into a barbershop wearing his uniform, full of decorations and ribbons. An empty sleeve dangled where he had lost his right arm in combat. Still, he was told: "We don't serve Japs here."[62]

Returning American veterans of Asian/Pacific Islander descent encountered discrimination in jobs, housing and receiving services. Raymond Lew, an Army veteran, recalled, "I was looking for a place to live around where Seattle Center is now. And the landlady said 'no,' but her rent sign was still up a week later. In 1951, one of my friends at work said, 'Hey, Ray, why don't you move up to the north end' where he lived. I said, 'Well, I don't know if they'll want me up there'…So he surveyed his neighborhood." Lew said 40 percent of the neighbors his friend surveyed wouldn't mind a Chinese American moving in, but 60 percent refused to have Lew as their neighbor.[63]

Because of their race, Asian Pacific American veterans also found that they could not join veterans' organizations like the American Legion and the Veterans of Foreign Wars (VFW). They had to establish their own groups, such as Seattle's Nisei Veterans Committee and the Cathy Post for Chinese American veterans.

Richard Naito, who served in the 442nd, applied three times in 1945 to become a member of a VFW Post in Spokane, Wash. Each time, he was refused because of his Japanese ancestry. Even with numerous letters of support from non-Japanese American veterans who praised the 442nd, Naito was not granted membership into the VFW Post until 1997, when current members offered it him and paid his dues.[64]

Benefits of Service

World War II gave Americans of Asian and Pacific Islander descent the chance to become American citizens. The 1,200 members of the 1st Filipino Infantry Regiment, who already lived in the states prior to the war, were sworn in as U.S. citizens at a mass naturalization ceremony on the parade ground at Camp Beale, Calif.[65] To express its appreciation to the Filipinos serving in the Philippines, the U.S. Congress in 1942 granted immediate citizenship to all who applied. However, since information about this opportunity was either lacking or confusing, many Filipino veterans missed their chance.[66]

After the United States granted independence to the Philippines in 1946, the U.S. government terminated that citizenship opportunity. Gen. MacArthur requested and was granted $200 million by the U.S. Congress to rebuild the Filipino Army and compensate Filipino veterans. Congress then passed the Rescission Act, denying full benefits to Filipino veterans and also limiting benefits to those who were wounded in action and to the families of those killed in the war. The Act also ruled that Filipino veterans would receive only half the pension granted U.S. veterans since Congress considered the Philippines to have a lower standard of living and that the Commonwealth Army was not officially part of the U.S. Army.[67] In 1990, Congress granted American citizenship rights to surviving veterans of the World War II Commonwealth Army of the Philippines. More than 20,000 Filipino veterans emigrated to the United States, with half settling in Los Angeles and hundreds moving to the Seattle area. Their struggle for full veteran's benefits, including a monthly pension, home loan guarantees, health care and education, continues today.[68]

Asian Pacific American servicemen accrued a particularly significant benefit: the ability to sponsor wives and family from Asian countries to the U.S. In 1946, U.S. immigration quotas stipulated that only 100 immigrants from the Philippines and India could enter the U.S.; 105 were allowed from China. None from Japan and Korea were allowed. A loophole through these stringent quotas was provided by the War Brides Act, which allowed Asian wives and children of

62 Takaki, *Strangers From a Different Shore*, p. 403.
63 Raymond Lew, interview with Carina A. del Rosario, March 3, 1999.
64 Richard Naito, interview with Linda Megumi Ando, Nov 11, 1998.
65 Takaki, *Strangers From a Different Shore*, p. 361.
66 Dorothy and Fred Cordova, interview with Mochizuki, Dec. 16, 1998.
67 Imbert Matthee, "Fighting a different battle: Filipinos say America has withheld veterans' benefits," *Seattle Post-Intelligencer*, Nov. 11, 1997; Lisa Charlie Ritts, "Time is running out," *International Examiner*, June 3-17, 1998.
68 Matthee, *Seattle-Post Intelligencer*, Nov. 11, 1997.

U.S. servicemen to enter without counting as part of the quota. The Filipino and Chinese American communities benefited the most from the War Brides Act, for the influx of women and children changed their predominantly bachelor societies. Over 7,000 Chinese war brides entered the U.S. between 1946 and 1953 after marrying Chinese American servicemen in China. Once they brought their new brides to America, Filipino American veterans then sent for their families.[69]

Seattle's Cathay Post helped returning Chinese American servicemen maneuver through the bureaucracy and bring their wives to America. "We asked a lot of them to file for citizenship," said David H. "Gobby" Woo, a World War II U.S. Air Force aerial gunner, former prisoner of war and one of the founders of Cathy Post. "We helped them with that, and we went and filed papers for them down in Immigration. And they went to China and they got married over there and came back."[70] The Korean War would later provide the means for about 17,000 Koreans to enter the U.S. between 1950 and 1965, since most of them were the spouses of American citizens.[71]

The Second Half of the Century:
Asian Pacific Americans' Service Broadens

The governments of the United States and the Republic of the Philippines entered into the Military Base Agreement of 1947. Provisions of that agreement allowed the U.S. Navy to be the only military branch and foreign country to have the right to enlist citizens of the Philippines into the U.S. Armed Forces. During the years of the Korean conflict, 1950-1953, U.S. Navy records show that 1,000 citizens of the Philippines joined the Navy in 1952, and the same number for 1953.[72]

When President Truman banned segregation from the U.S. Armed Forces in 1947, the end of segregated military units also meant the end of one way to count the number of Asian Pacific Americans who served in military conflicts to come. During the Korean conflict, when U.S. forces joined in a United Nations effort to repel North Korean invaders of South Korea, Asian Pacific Americans served in all branches of the U.S. military. Many Japanese American MIS veterans of World War II were called back into active duty and sent to Korea. Robert Wada, president of the Japanese American Korean War Veterans, discovered

records confirming that 246 Japanese American members of the U.S. Armed Forces were killed in action in Korea. Seventy percent of those killed were of Japanese ancestry from Hawaii. He estimates that over 1,000 Japanese Americans alone served in the Korean war.[73]

As in previous wars, Asian Pacific Americans served in various capacities during the Korean War. Three distinguished themselves with acts of bravery and were awarded Congressional Medals of Honor.

Beginning the night of Apr. 24, 1951, Cpl. Hiroshi "Hershey" Miyamura, of Gallup, N.M., and with the Army's 3rd Infantry Division, fought off an attack on American positions near Taejon-Ni, Korea, by leaping out of his shelter with a bayonet and killing about 10 of the enemy in hand-to-hand combat. He then administered first aid to wounded GIs and directed their evacuation. When another assault commenced, Miyamura fired a machine gun until ammunition had been expended. He then ordered his squad to withdraw and stayed behind until his machine gun gave out. Miyamura bayoneted enemy soldiers breaking through fortifications, then made his way to a second machine gun and assisted in firing that gun. With the American positions about to be overrun, Miyamura ordered his men to fall back while he covered their retreat with the machine gun. Miyamura alone killed more than 50 of the enemy until his ammunition was gone and he was severely wounded.[74]

Originally from Honolulu, Hawaii, Sgt. Leroy A. Mendonca was also with the Army's 3rd Infantry Division after a fierce fight for Hill 586 near Chich-on, Korea, July 4, 1951. That night, a superior enemy force attacked. Mendonca's 1st Platoon was ordered to withdraw to a secondary line of defense, but Mendonca volunteered to remain behind. He covered his platoon's retreat, exhausting all the ammunition in his weapons and throwing all his grenades. Using his bayonet and his rifle like a club, Mendonca accounted for 37 enemy casualties until he was mortally wounded. His actions stalled the enemy assault and protected the platoon's withdrawal. The platoon regrouped and repelled the enemy attack, enabling American forces to keep the vital hilltop position.[75]

69 Takaki, *Strangers From a Different Shore*, p. 417.
70 David H. "Gobby" Woo, interview with Ron Chew, Oct. 29 and Nov. 2, 1990.
71 Takaki, *Strangers From a Different Shore*, p. 417.
72 Flores, "A Historical Account of the Filipino Experience in the United States Navy," p. 11, p. 41.
73 Robert Wada, interview with Ken Mochizuki, Jan. 6, 1999.
74 George Lang, Raymond L. Collins, Gerard F. White, *Medal of Honor Recipients* 1863-1994, New York: Facts on File, Inc., 1995, p. 635.

Another Hawaiian, PFC Hebert K. Pililaau, was posthumously awarded the Congressional Medal of Honor for his one-man stand near Pia-Ri, Korea, on Sept. 17, 1951. His platoon, part of the Army's 2nd Infantry Division holding on to key terrain on "Heartbreak Ridge," repelled waves of attacks by enemy soldiers until ammunition was exhausted. The platoon withdrew to a new position. Volunteering to stay behind and cover, Pililaau fought off the enemy with his automatic weapon and grenades, then fought hand-to-hand with a trench knife and his bare fists until being mortally wounded. Forty enemy dead were counted in the area he defended.[76]

Many Asian Pacific Americans also served in the rear, providing crucial support to the soldiers on the front line. Some coordinated needed supplies while others tended to the wounded in medical units. "You saw some pretty bad injuries," said Stan Tsujikawa, who worked in a Mobile Army Surgical Hospital (MASH) unit. "Naturally, most of us were not used to seeing open wounds and the dead and amputees. I was the type that…probably would have fainted. And in order to be able to get used to it – surgery was just another tent right next to the post-op – when I had time, I used to go into the surgery and just watch them do everything until I got sick. Then I'd run outside until everything felt better and then I'd go right back in there. I kept doing that until I got to the point where I could stand seeing all that blood and amputations. It's not that pretty."[77]

The Korean conflict ended in 1953 when a truce was declared, keeping Korea divided into a North and South. According to the U.S. Department of Defense, "A military problem that remains today is that no peace treaty has ever been signed to end the Korean War. The two sides talk to each other regularly around a table in a shed at the 38th parallel in the city of Panmunjom."[78]

Lorea T. Acuszaar, (1930-1993)
"I was a San Diego Alumni scholar to University of California, Berkeley, in 1952. At the time the Korean War was on so many of us wanted to get involved. I took a direct commission and became an occupational therapist with the U.S. Women's Medical Specialist Corps. It was an exciting opportunity."
–Courtesy of Karen and Charles Johnstone.

75 *The Congressional Medal of Honor: the Names, the Deeds*, p. 216.
76 Ibid., p. 226.
77 Stan Tsujikawa, interview with Pei Pei Sung, Feb. 6, 1999.
78 DEOMI, "Asian-Pacific Heritage Month 1999," p. 19.

Southeast Asia:
Looking Like the Enemy

Soon after the stalemate in Korea, the U.S. continued its battle against communism – this time in Southeast Asia. The U.S. military secretly started to fight the North Vietnamese Army, its Vietcong guerrilla allies in South Vietnam, and the Pathet Lao forces in Laos. The U.S. Central Intelligence Agency supported governments opposed to the communists. By the early 1960s, the CIA and U.S. military advisors – elite Army Special Forces and Navy Sea, Air and Land teams (SEALs) – recruited, trained and supplied members of Southeast Asian indigenous tribes to aid South Vietnam in its fight against the North. Most of those forming these U.S.-backed irregular forces were from the Montagnard, Meo, Mien and Nung peoples of Vietnam, Laos and Cambodia.[79]

U.S. policymakers directing the war in Southeast Asia concluded that military advisors weren't enough and sent more and more U.S. troops into South Vietnam. By the mid-'60s, young Americans found themselves subject to a draft to supply more manpower in Vietnam.

The 1990 Census counted 88,118 Asian Pacific American Vietnam veterans.[80] As the oral histories included in this book will show, Asian Pacific Americans were everything from regular infantrymen and sailors, elite Army Rangers, Marines, Air Force commandos and pilots to typists for the generals or health inspectors for the troops.

Some Asian Pacific American Vietnam veterans say their experiences were like any other soldier, sailor or airman doing their job, and felt they were treated accordingly. Others recall being caught in the peculiar situation of being ethnically Asian and fighting Asians in an Asian war. Sometimes their ethnicity was an advantage that saved their lives. In other instances, what they looked like placed them in dire jeopardy. Some were nearly killed by their own people, or were brought before recruits in basic training to be used as an example of "what the enemy looks like."

Ron Chinn, an Army Ranger who left Vietnam with the rank of captain, recounted his basic training: "They constantly called me 'gook.' My name wasn't Chinn anymore. Another one could be Pvt. Swanson, and I'd be Pvt. Gook."[81]

In the front lines, American soldiers of Asian/Pacific Islander descent had to be careful to identify themselves, lest they be mistaken by their fellow soldiers as the enemy. Lorenzo Silvestre, a Marine in Vietnam, recalled, "Most of the patrol goes back at night before daylight. But, in my case, I don't go back until 10 o'clock in the morning – make sure it's full daylight before I go back because, me being Oriental and exactly the same as Vietnamese... Long before I'm coming into the perimeter, I was yelling so I wouldn't be mistaken as the enemy. Basically, it put me in a position that it's easy to get killed."[82]

Even while serving stateside during the Vietnam War, Asian Pacific American women shared similar experiences. During July 4, 1970, Teresita Iriarte Coalson, who served in Army intelligence, was watching fireworks in an open field "and the next thing I know I'm being beaten by someone who is calling me a gook." Although she recalls being assaulted other times because she was a woman, Coalson said this instance "was not because of who I was, it was who he thought I was. When you're having a flashback as he was, I was just a gook."[83]

–Courtesy of JoAnn L. Oligario, 1963.

79 John S. Bowman, *The World Almanac of the Vietnam War*, New York: World Almanac, 1985, pp. 440-469.
80 DEOMI, "Asian-Pacific American Heritage Month 1999," p. 20.
81 Ron Chinn, interview with Ken Mochizuki, Nov. 9, 1998.
82 Lorenzo "Larry" Silvestre, interview with Jose Velasquez, Jan. 27, 1999.
83 Teresita Iriarte Coalson, interview with Ken Mochizuki, Nov. 12, 1998.

During World War II, Asian Pacific American women served with U.S. military units such as the Women's Army Corps and Women Air Force Service Pilots. Approximately 7,000 women – including Asian Pacific Americans – served in Vietnam. They were U.S. military officers or professional nurses before the war. They not only cared for U.S. soldiers, but also Vietnamese civilians and prisoners of war.[84]

They often experienced sexism and the same racism as their male counterparts. Lily Jean Lee Adams, a Chinese American combat nurse with the 12th Evacuation Hospital in Vietnam, remembered walking around her military compound in jeans and civilian wear and being crudely propositioned by American soldiers who had mistaken her for a prostitute. "It really hurt inside that I had just spent 12 hours treating their buddies, and they thought I was just some Vietnamese whore."[85]

Despite the maltreatment from some fellow soldiers, Asian Pacific American soldiers proved their dedication in the Vietnam War. Two more Asian Pacific Americans received Congressional Medals of Honor while fighting in this war.

Sgt. 1st Class Rodney J.T. Yano, of Kona, Hawaii, flew as a crew chief aboard a command-and-control helicopter during action with the 11th Armored Cavalry Regiment near Bien Hao, Republic of Vietnam, on Jan. 1, 1969. Yano's helicopter unit attacked the enemy entrenched in dense jungle. Out in the open and in the face of intense small arms and anti-aircraft fire, Yano delivered suppressive fire with a helicopter door gun and marked enemy positions with smoke and white phosphorous grenades, enabling troop commanders to direct accurate artillery fire against enemy emplacements. One of the grenades Yano handled exploded prematurely, covering him with burning phosphorous.. Flaming fragments from the grenade set off ammunition and supplies within the helicopter. With dense smoke filling the helicopter, the pilot began to lose control. Yano, with only one good arm and partially blinded by the exploding grenade, hurled blazing ammunition from the helicopter, inflicting more wounds on himself. He persisted until his helicopter was out of danger. Yano saved the rest of his helicopter crew, but lost his own life.[86]

Army Cpl. Terry Teruo Kawamura, from Wahiawa, Oahu, was stationed with the 173rd Engineer Company, 173rd Airborne Brigade at Camp Radcliff in the Republic of Vietnam, March 20, 1969. An enemy demolition team infiltrated his unit's quarters area and opened fire with automatic weapons. Under intense fire, Kawamura ran for his weapon. An explosion tore a hole in the roof of his quarters. Running to a door to return fire, he saw another explosive charge thrown through the hole in the roof, which dropped to the floor. Although Kawamura was in position to escape from the explosion, he shouted a warning to two fellow soldiers, then wheeled around and threw himself on the charge. By absorbing the explosion with his own body, he saved several members of his unit.[87]

Surviving Vietnam veterans say they continue to struggle with what they experienced during the war. "You feel guilty 'cause your friends got killed and you didn't get killed," said Pete Sua, who was in the Marine Corps. "And then you turn around and you start feeling guilty because you killed somebody's father or somebody's son. I'm still processing, still there with it."[88] Like Sua, suffer from Post Traumatic Stress Syndrome (PTSD), a mental illness only identified after thousands of veterans complained of nightmares, flashbacks, difficulty being close to people and other symptoms that prevented them from resuming their lives as civilians. "I felt more suicidal after the war," said Howard Kim, who was a demolition specialist in the Army. "I went and sought counseling when I first got out in the sixties. And I didn't know what I really needed. They didn't know what it was that I had. Why am I reliving these things over and over again? It's emotional scars that stay there. Some people say scars don't hurt, but there are some scars that hurt. The emotional kind does."[89]

Influenced by news media coverage of the war, the American public intensified pressure on the U.S. government to pull out of Vietnam. Some returning veterans were greeted not by ticker-tape parades, as their fathers were after World War II. Instead, they were confronted by protesters. "It's funny being a veteran; you see both sides," said Mike Higashi, who worked in preventative medicine with the Army. "One side, you want to support the guys who are in Vietnam because you already were there and you know that you don't choose to be there, but you're

84 Ken Mochizuki and Lily Adams, unpublished paper, 1989, pp.12-15.
85 Victor Merina, "The glory and pain of fighting for your country," Rice, Vol. 1, No. 9, April 1988, p. 37.
86 The Congressional Medal of Honor: the Names, the Deeds, p. 167.
87 Ibid., p. 87.
88 Pete Sua, interview with Michael Park, Nov. 12, 1998.
89 Howard Kim, interview with Debbie Abe, Nov. 14, 1998.

there. But on the other hand, you realize that the ones who are protesting are also shortening the war."[90] The U.S. pulled out of Vietnam in April 1975 when the Republic of Vietnam fell to North Vietnamese and Vietcong forces.

Since the war in Vietnam, Asian Pacific Americans have continued to serve in the U.S. military and its armed conflicts. During the U.S. Armed Forces' 1983 operation to rescue American students and fight Cuban soldiers in Grenada, 18 U.S. soldiers were killed in action. Among them was an Army Ranger from Seattle, Mark O. Yamane. When Iraqi dictator Saddam Hussein invaded the neighboring country of Kuwait and annexed it as a part of Iraq in 1990, Asian Pacific Americans served in every facet of the U.S. Armed Forces during the Persian Gulf War of 1991. U.S. forces, along with its allies, drove Iraqi forces out of Kuwait in 100 hours. No exact counts of Asian Pacific Americans serving in the Persian Gulf War are available because no racially segregated units have existed since World War II to make possible the tracking of ethnicity within the U.S. Armed Forces, and because the Census that would collect this data has not yet been conducted.

Mark O. Yamane (1963 – 1983), 1981.
—Courtesy of Yamane Family.

A More Complete History

Despite their long history of military service, even Asian Pacific Americans are not aware of the thousands of other soldiers, sailors and airmen and women of Asian/Pacific Islander descent. "When I was in Korea, I thought I was the only Japanese American there," said Robert Wada, who served in the Marine Corps.[91] Asian Pacific Americans have played significant roles in every facet of American history – in the military, in labor and civil rights struggles, in science and the arts. By learning of these contributions, all Americans can have a more complete and complex view of our history and our country's heroes and heroines.

90 Mike Higashi, interview with Pei Pei Sung, Feb. 5, 1999.
91 Wada, interview with Mochizuki, Jan. 6, 1999.

A Different BATTLE:
Stories of Asian Pacific American Veterans

BY DIRECT WIRE FROM

WESTERN UNION

CLASS OF SERVICE

his is a full-rate
gram or Cable-
a unless its de-
d character is in-
ced by a suitable
ool above or pre-
ng the address.

A. N. WILLIAMS
PRESIDENT

NEWCOMB CARLTON
CHAIRMAN OF THE BOARD

J. C. W
FIRST VICE

ng time shown in the date line on telegrams and day letters is STANDARD TIME at point of origin. Time of recei

P106 40 GOVT WASHINGTON DC 2 514P VIA H

AN CHIN=

2016 12 AVE SOUTH

SECRETARY OF WAR DESIRES ME TO INFORM

CHIN, WILLIAM IS PRISONER OF WAR OF GE

Fred ABE

Vietnam War
Army, 9th Infantry Division, 1956-1983
Command Sergeant Major, E-9

I went in the Army in 1956. I should have gotten out in 1958 but I re-enlisted…because I went on leave one time. I didn't want to go, but…Capt. Lorus Dall Jewkes bought me the plane ticket to go home. Alyce and Joe [family members] sent him the money back 'cause Joe had his stomach out and couldn't go out and harvest the crops. I had to go home and help harvest. Capt. Jewkes said, "You're going home." He went down and bought the plane ticket. Being as he was from Spanish Forks, Utah, near Salt Lake City, he knew what farming was.

When I got back, I was reassigned and went over to 2nd Armored Division. I put up with them for about a month and found that wasn't that great. So I told Capt. Jewkes, "I'm ready to come back." They re-enlisted me and put me back in the same unit. I liked the military by that time. I was already a non-commissioned officer. As long as I did the job good, I was treated with respect, dignity. People looked up to me for what I accomplished.

[While stationed at Fort Hood, Texas], I remember there were a lot of veterans in Temple. They'd ask me, "Are you a Jap?" I figured, boy, here I'm going to get it again. They said, "Come here." I went over there and they'd get me drunk. They'd be telling me all these stories about how a Japanese American unit saved them. It wasn't

Uncle Sam does a lot of good things, but boy, when it comes to veterans, they're stuck out in the middle of left field.

'til later on in life that I found out the 442nd regiment went in and saved them. I didn't know that. I just thought, boy, these guys are something else, treating me this way. They invited me to their house, to dinner.

On the frontlines

In Vietnam, one time we were surrounded by Vietcong and we couldn't get in or out. So here comes a radio message in by teletype. Col. Pears come over and said, "I want to talk to you." I thought, "Oh, I had done something wrong again." He sat me down and told me, "Your dad died." We were surrounded by Vietcong. I couldn't get in or out. I drafted up a message. They sent it back to Alyce. I said I'd pay for part of the funeral and that I wouldn't be able to come home. I was more worried about what was going to happen to us. As it happened, the infantry came and got all of the Vietcong out of our way.

I was a first sergeant and I had my own fire base. We were pretty good at first. We used to get hit by mortars and rockets from the Vietcong all the time. Then one night, I was walking around, I saw this guy, Cannon from Texas, lying up on the berm, what they call the gun pit. On top of one of the sandbags was Cannon lying up there. I said, "Cannon, get up. Get your ass off that berm." He didn't move or nothing. So I told the medic, "Come up here and check this guy out. What's wrong with him?" He said, "He's dead." I immediately got the doctor down there. He said, "This guy died of an overdose." During my tour, we only lost one guy. That was Cannon.

I wiped clean that fire base. I brought in search dogs. I brought in MPs (military police). I had this whole fire base searched and found cocaine, heroin, marijuana, hashish. I found all these bottles of whiskey and stuff. I set this 55-gallon drum in the middle of this fire base. I dumped all this stuff inside it and then I poured gas on it.

They [soldiers on base] started doing things then, just minor things at first. One time, they put a C-4 charge [plastic explosives] on me. I had what they called a hooch. They stuck the C-4 under my doorway. They were going to blow me away. When that detonator went off between me and the generator shop, I knew someone in the generator shop had set it off because he had to be there to squeeze this thing to make it go off.

When I came home the first time, protesters were spittin' at me in the San Francisco International Airport. I was indoctrinated when we came back to Oakland Army Terminal at Travis Air Force Base. They told us, "Don't get hepped over all this protesting." They wouldn't turn you loose without telling you what to expect. They give you a good indoctrination and tell you not to get into fights. I just ignored the people spitting. Inside, I felt like running up there and choking the guy. Like I told this one long-haired freak, "Keep it up buddy. You won't have no long hair when I get a hold of you." He took off.

I thought when we first went over there, we had a mission and a good life to protect. We really had a good indoctrination about Vietnam, how the Vietnamese just needed more power to fight Communist forces. But after I went over there and saw what they were doing and old Gen. Westmoreland playing games, I said, "What a waste!" All these guys dying. I used to see a lot of body bags. And I'd say, "Why are we doing all this for them?" The second time when I was first sergeant, I saw a bigger, broader view of it. I read a lot of things. I said, "Boy, big business is getting rich here and the GI is just being used as a sucker."

A military career

When I came back to Fort Lewis later in my service, I was assigned as command sergeant major of 1st Battalion, 84th Field Artillery, 9th Infantry Division. Gen. Cavazos told me it needed to be straightened out. Then after that, Gen. Cavazos said, "You're going to the NCO Academy" 'cause he's having problems there. It was rated the worst NCO Academy in the U.S. Army. The next year we were inspected and rated first by what they call Training and Doctrine Command. We were rated the best NCO Academy in Forces Command, which is the largest command in the Army, and the next year, best in the U.S. Army.

When it comes to veterans, once you do your time, as far as Uncle Sam is concerned: Stuff it, to hell with it. I got Agent Orange while in Vietnam. The United States government says, "We don't recognize it. Go to Aetna Insurance Company's Agent Orange program." So I went to them. They gave me $10,000. Then I went back to the VA and they said, "You don't have what we recognize in Agent Orange as a disability so we're not going to give you anything. But we're going to take care of you for all this other stuff. But as far as getting additional money for having Agent Orange, we won't pay for it 'cause it's not cancer." As far as I'm concerned, Uncle Sam does a lot of good things, but boy, when it comes to veterans, they're stuck out in the middle of left field.

Interviewed by Debby Abe.

Antonio AGUON

Vietnam War
Army, 25th Division, 14th Infantry, 1962-1984
1st Sergeant

My father was a farmer. He raised us the old fashioned way which is, you're parents are right, you listen to your parents and you do what you are told. That's the reason why I did not have any difficulties in the military because it was instilled in us to obey your parents.

I was very impressed about the Marines. I looked highly on them as the people who really protected our island [Guam during World War II]. When I was in high school, we had this Guamanian guy who was a captain in the Marine Corps who came to our high school. They were playing the Drum and Bugle Corps. I was very impressed and I always wanted to be in the military. When I finished my high school, I didn't enlist, but I applied to be in the Marines. And then I applied to be in the Air Force and then the Army. But before I did that, when I graduated from high school, I went and took the civil service test. I held a grudge with the military because when I took that test, I scored in the high 90s, but the policy or the rule on the island was that veterans have priority over civilians. So that's one of the reasons why I joined the military.

I was with the 25th division, 14th Infantry in the Army. What really opened my heart and my mind to the military was when my father…was

We never experienced the difficulties of discrimination. When you are in the combat zone, you bond together.

very ill. I went home when the Red Cross sent a message that my father's very ill and he's likely to live no more than six months. So while I was home…I wrote back to the Department of the Army and asked them if I could be stationed in Guam. As a private, I asked myself, "Who am I to ask a four-star general that I want to stay with my dad?" At any rate, my request was granted. So about a month later, my father passed away. After everything was settled down, I went back to my unit in Schoffield Barracks…

Surviving Vietnam

When I graduated from basic and AIT (Advanced Intelligence Training), they assigned me to the motor pool to take care of vehicles. I really didn't like that because I always got greasy hands, dirty clothes. So I asked my boss, my platoon sergeant, if I could transfer to the mortar platoon. We were out in the field exercise and we didn't see very much action when we were practicing war games – mostly sitting down. When they call in for fire support, that's when we start doing our math and loading up the ammunition. So my friend and I talked about it and we wanted to transfer because the infantry was always going out some places. So we went to the company commander and we told him that we liked that infantry and he looked at us and asked us why do we like it. When you're young and all that, you like to move around all the time. He assigned us to an infantry platoon. That's when we grew up.

In 1963, I went to Vietnam. What made me stay there was one reason only…my good buddy, Jim. He went back to the United States, he stayed in Oakland, Calif., for less than a month and then he was shipped right back to

Vietnam. Then two or three weeks later, they got hit by a whole lot of forces, North Vietnamese, and he got killed. And when I got the message that he got killed I said, "No, I better stay here. I better keep extending over here until everything gets settled down." If I leave Vietnam, that's well and fine, but the crisis was still very active at that time. He came right back again. And then to come back to a different zone, I-Corps. There were four corps over there and I was in IV-Corps. I-Corps is the closest to North Vietnam. We were down in IV-Corps by the delta. From there, he went back to the States, and from the States back to Vietnam [and was moved closer to the border]. It kind of scared me. I still wanted to see my little one back in Guam. I should stay there because I was in a good location.

When I was over there, I know how to speak Vietnamese because I went to language school. Whenever we're out on the village, just about every time, you see the Vietnamese talking to me. And then villagers would find out later from the interpreter that I'm not Vietnamese. I was just a boy, a young boy. I looked like a Vietnamese, and I spoke their language a little bit, and our culture was almost similar. In the unit, my first medic was a Black guy. The second one was a White guy. And then the armor advisor was a Black guy. And the other minority was a Mexican guy. He's young too, like me – don't care about nothin.' We treated the natives with the same respect that we wanted them to treat us. We never experienced the difficulties of discrimination. When you are in the combat zone, you bond together. I'll cover your back and you cover my back. Maybe because it's just a few groups of people out there in no man's land and we have to take care of each other.

My first encounter with discrimination was when we were out for Guard Mount. If you get picked, you get to stay with the colonel for three days. On a few occasions, I missed the assignment not because I gave the wrong response to the officer, but because I was a foreigner. I ignored that. When I went to Alaska, we took the Army test annually for getting a group of people to meet the objective and this guy missed his objective. His group missed completely and… he was reprimanded for missing his objective. There should be a record of that. When it came to promotion time, he was with me in the promotion. So what does that mean? This was a White guy. What does that mean? But if you don't look at it, if you just ignore that, you'll be okay. Sure you got promoted side by side with a guy that has a goof up. Hooray for him. See, in the military, it's not what you know, it's who you know.

As I look at the United States and Iraq and I think back to what we did in Vietnam and the Korean War, why didn't they negotiate instead of having people lose their lives because of a disagreement between two countries? They could have done it a better way by coming to the table, both of them, and negotiating. Why didn't they do that in the beginning to avoid all these lives that were lost, all this hatred and a lot of soldiers missing?

Interviewed by Firia Aguon and Pei Pei Sung.

Aguon (third from left) with his Mobile Advisory Team in South Vietnam, 1963.
—Courtesy of Antonio Aguon.

Mariano Bello ANGELES

World War II
Army, 1st Filipino Infantry, 1943-1947
Sergeant, Technician 3rd Grade

I arrived here in June 1927, at Victoria, Canada. We stayed there for one night and the next day we came to Seattle. It was always my ambition to go abroad. I had a friend over here, a townmate who was in Iowa during that time, who used to write to us over there in the Philippines about America. I was still a young man when the missionaries were boarding in our home and they told us what America is, what kind of people they have and what government they have…They describe America as a "dry" country and there is no drinking or something like that. They also say democracy and equality, justice and liberty and freedom – those are the American teachings there.

So when I came here I was surprised that the first person I saw was a drunkard on the street. And then at the same time, when I went and looked for a room or apartment, here I had a hard time. We had friends here already, other townmates of ours who came before me. I don't like to go and bother them so I have to go and look for my own room. Where I like to go, they don't like. Like the Olympic Hotel or something like that. They didn't like Orientals during those times. So again I like to eat, so I went to the restaurant to eat. Here again, it is disappointment that I really come across. And the first day, they don't like to serve me. So I said to myself, "This is America."

I worked and went to school from 1928 to 1930. Then I quit and I took a job again in the ship with the intention to go back to the Philippines. That is during the severity of the Depression and, at the same time, I did not like this place. From the experience I have – that's why. I look for a job in the ship and I was able to take a job in the ship as a captain's clerk or captain boy. They give me $45 as a wage each month at that time. The ship will travel around the world. I was very happy to get it but it happened that I was not a good sailor and got seasick. Got sick so then they dropped me in San Francisco.

I did not wait for my induction. I was going into the military because the Philippines was involved.

1st Filipino Infantry

I enlisted. I did not wait for my induction. I was just going into the military because the Philippines was involved. Then when I was in the Army, I was assigned on the medical detachment of the 1st Filipino Infantry. Before World War II, we Filipinos were fighting to become a citizen. The Philippine and the U.S. government wouldn't give us that privilege except those who already are in the service. Those were the ones who were eligible only but us here, as a private citizen, we were not able to. Then during the World War II, when we were in the Army… then you can ask. In fact, they try to force you to get American citizenship. That was the thing that I fought. I resented it. Why do they have to become an American citizen now? But only they give it to the servicemen, see? Now I resented that. I refused to become an American citizen. When we were private citizens, we asked before and they didn't like us. In fact, they branded us. They even described us as barbarous. And why only the soldiers? So they mean to say that when my future is to die, that is the time when they give me the privilege to become American, so hell no.

How I came back, I was discharged in Fort Lewis, and came back to Seattle. I went back to Mrs. Perkins' place to be janitor again but different already. Different because there is a union and also different management already. I tried to take a job under the GI program, something like that, and I went and applied to the City Light, to the public health but they don't hire me. Frederick and Nelson, no, they still have that prejudice or discrimination. And the same attitude just after the war, the same attitude as before. Prejudice among Americans towards the Filipinos just gradually, year by year, became lax. But after the war – the same. One year after that, still the same. Then sooner or later, we were able to get our wives here, especially the service wives. Those men who came over here with the war brides now. They have no such trouble about discrimination anymore.

Interviewed by Cynthia Mejia-Guidici,
courtesy of Filipino American National Historical Society (FANHS).

Mariano Angeles and war bride, Angeles V. Angeles
before re-settling in the United States, 1947.
–Courtesy of Angeles Family.

Warren CHAN

World War II
Army, 75th Joint Assault Signal Company, 1942-1945
Technician 4th Grade, T-4

Sept. 25, 1942, I volunteered for the Army so that, as distinct from a draftee, I could pick the particular branch of service I desired. I chose the Signal Corps as being the safest during war time.

After basic training and radio operator's school, I was assigned to the 75th Joint Assault Signal Company. Following six weeks of practicing assault beach landings, the company was attached to the 7th Infantry Division to retake Attu, the westernmost island in the Aleutian chain which extends westward from Alaska across the northern Pacific Ocean toward Russia. Early in the war, Japan captured the two westernmost islands: Attu and Kiska. Most Americans were not aware that this happened.

Since I was of Chinese ancestry, the company commander was very aware of the likelihood that trigger-happy soldiers might mistake me for the enemy; so I was assigned to the headquarters combat team that would not be assigned to an infantry battalion but remain with the reserve force in a troop transport in Adak harbor, at least 100 miles from Attu. However, this protective assignment was not afforded me in later campaigns. I did not see Attu until the last desperate banzai charge of the Japanese had resulted in their annihilation.

A constant problem in the Aleutians is the fog. In making the assault, the landing craft (LCVPs) are lowered onto the ocean waters while some five

Since I was of Chinese ancestry, the company commander was very aware of the likelihood that trigger happy soldiers might mistake me for the enemy.

miles or so from the beach. The men with the gear climb down cargo nets into the LCVPs, which, when fully loaded, would commence circling for as long as several hours until the signal is given to charge in a strung-out wave towards the beach. However, with the fog and hour of circling, some of the coxswains weren't sure which direction the beach was.

Aug. 15, 1943, three months after Attu, the assault landing on Kiska occurred. Like Attu, Kiska is mountainous, with ridges coming to the water's edge, separating the beaches where different battalions landed. As each group moved inland, they were not aware that the several ridges would come together, and in the fog each thought the other was the enemy and would shoot at each other. The next morning, I was on duty in a snow jeep – a tracked vehicle – when bodies were carried down to the beach. I counted 17 bodies. So from our beach, 17 men were killed. Later, we were told by members of our company, who were attached to the reserve force, that they had been advised the day before we hit the beaches that the Japanese had likely vacated the island earlier. Not a word of this was given to the landing force. I thought, "How stupid can our leaders be?"

From the fog, cold and dampness of the Aleutians, the 75th was transferred to the South Pacific – hot and humid. First, there was a landing on Makin Island in the Gilbert Islands, which I did not take part in, as I was again assigned to headquarters team. Next was Kwajalein in the Marshall Islands, which I did take part in. This was called an artillery-man's dream campaign. I landed the day before the main landing, with an artillery group on an adjacent island several miles offshore of the main island of Kwajalein. By five in the afternoon, 50 pieces of artillery were in place. I had just fallen asleep in preparation to taking the night watch, when the whole island erupted. The bombardment of the main island had started and the artillery literally "walked" their shells up an island four miles long and two miles wide at its widest. By the next morning, when the main assault force landed, there was virtually no resistance as the garrison of 5,000 men, including Prime Minister Tojo's son, had been wiped out, at a cost of possibly one American soldier.

On Jan. 9, 1945, an assault landing took place in Lingayen Gulf on Luzon, Philippines. The first wave landed at about 8 a.m. My combat team was aboard an LST – landing ship tank – a 400-foot craft of shallow draft, capable of transporting a company of armored tanks, or as, in this instance, a battery of artillery. Orders for our LST to land came around noon. So here we are, steaming full speed toward shore when suddenly, enemy artillery fire started landing in front of our ship. I was shocked to hear the ship's captain order: "Stop all engines. Reverse all engines. I'm not going to have my ship sunk." The ship slowly backed away. I thought, "Surely, this captain will be up for court martial!" The Army needed the artillery ashore to fire back at the artillery shooting at us.

Our second run at the beach occurred at 5 p.m. This

Four Brothers in the Philippines

Four sons of Mr. and Mrs. J. Chan, 335 23rd Avenue North, are now in the Philippines. Ship Fitter Bertram Chan is in the Seabees, with the 78th Construction Battalion. Sergeant Warren Chan, a radio man, is in the 75th Joint Assault Signal Company. Private Quentin Chan is in the Headquarters Detachment of the 85th Chemical Battalion. Radioman Leslie Chan is in a Navy Communication Unit.

BERTRAM CHAN

WARREN CHAN

QUENTIN CHAN

LESLIE CHAN

–Courtesy of Warren Chan

time, we landed, notwithstanding some intermittent artillery fire against us. This was my first experience with being on the receiving end of artillery fire. But it was worse after we landed. All night long, the shells came whistling in – scared the daylights out of me. I could hear the whistling sound coming toward me, then followed by an explosion, then the fluttering of shrapnel, all around. If I were hit by a piece of shrapnel, it could tear me apart. The artillery we landed with would fire a barrage, and, as they were reloading, an answering barrage would come whistling in. It got so bad that I was hoping our guns would shut down, and then, maybe, the opposing guns would, too! If this was a classic artillery duel, it was too scary for me. I couldn't sleep. When daylight came, the

enemy artillery fire ceased. One of my friends had slept through all this firing and didn't know what had happened. I said, "See that shrapnel? That was flying through the air." "Oh my Lord," he said. "Is that what was going on?" Then that night he couldn't sleep.

April 1, 1945 was Easter Sunday. There was an assault landing on Okinawa. This was a bitterly fought campaign. When Japanese troops were driven to the southern end of the island, rather than surrender they – along with thousands of civilians – leaped off the cliffs to their death into the sea, a hundred feet or more below. This I did not see personally, but I saw on film later. Our company had already returned to Luzon to help train a regular infantry division to become an amphibious assault beach landing division to make a Nov. 1, 1945 landing on Honshu. Each of our combat teams was attached to a regiment of infantry and made practice landings on the beaches in Lingayen Gulf. We were also there to prepare for dissolution of the 75th Joint Assault Signal Company, as more than three-quarters of us had 85 points or more – the minimum under the Army's point system for discharge from military service. The war in Europe had ended and the Army needed much fewer men to continue the war against Japan.

While aboard a troop transport off Lingayen Gulf making practice landings, the ship's radio operators were betting $1,000 the war would be over in 48 hours. Evidently, they had picked up some radio communication we didn't know about. "Oh gosh," I thought. "They're crazy, betting $1,000?" I had just received my orders to report to a replacement center in Manila for discharge. A day or two after the practice landing, I was in a replacement center in Manila undergoing orientation for discharge when news came of the dropping of the atomic bomb on Hiroshima.

Interviewed by Ron Chew and John D. Pai

Ark G. CHIN

World War II
Army, 299th Infantry Regiment, 100th Infantry Division, 1942-1946
Sergeant

Physically, I was just in really bad shape, because I was 5'10", and I was 119 pounds. Can you imagine? When they drafted me, before I went in for a physical exam, I ate a lot of bananas so I wouldn't be rejected because I was under weight. I went in, and at that time my dad was being discharged because he had this ulcer. So he had preceded me into service. He must have gone in about 1942, or very early on in '43.

Through that basic training, because now I was sleeping regular, eating regular, I got up to 135 pounds! The training, though, really built you up physically and mentally made you tough! You are trained then to react to commands. If they say "charge," they hope you'll charge without saying why and raising questions.

I was always pretty much the only Asian. In the beginning, in basic training, there was some sense of prejudice but as we stayed together they found out that we all have the same aspirations. We all have the love for the family and so that became a blur and the war helped create a true kinship for each other.

I was always pretty much the only Asian. In the beginning... there was some sense of prejudice but as we stayed together, they found out that we all have the same aspirations.

you know you're going in to fill spots vacated by people who were killed or wounded. We were all pretty raw but we knew each other.

[We were trying to get ashore to Italy by land craft] when the "Bed Check Charlie" came over. That's a nickname for the German bomber that they send every night just to drop a few bombs. So here we were, it wasn't full and you couldn't sit down and standard operating procedures were that you have to cast off, get away from the big ship, and so we were circling around in the harbor for hours with these huge packs on our backs. We had something like 80 pounds on our backs, rifle and all that stuff and you couldn't sit down. So finally, we landed and it was raining. And then they marched us out to what they call a bivouac area. And then we put up tents. The field was muddy but by then we were so tired, we didn't care. We just dropped off and slept.

I can remember that first attack. The fear was just a constant companion. On the attack, some of those guys, they couldn't get up and go. When I was young, it is what you would call a tough life. So you learn to endure things and that, I think, helped me survive in the war. I later thought about it, there was another element: I sure was not going to be the guy that brings shame to my race.

One memory in particular that really bothered me: He was a replacement, a fellow named Wright and he was already married and had a daughter. I used to talk with him about that. And then he hit a land

I went overseas as a private first class. Lucky thing is that we went overseas as a division. A lot of those guys went overseas as a replacement, so you can imagine how frightening that was to enter the war totally raw and

mine. I felt terrible about that, I was thinking about his daughter. The person I could talk to was the medic. Our medic, he was older, meaning he was in his 30s, and so I was in my early 20s. He was like a father figure; he was a steady influence. He'd just kind of pat you on the back and say, "It's okay, it's okay." And pretty soon you had to rely on your inner self because you realize that everyone else is dealing with the same thing.

I can still remember the night there was maybe 20 percent, or 25 percent of the original company was still together. Some were wounded once or twice, but nevertheless still there. The captain of the company was our platoon leader. And the first lieutenant was my squad leader, so I knew both of them very well. By the time we were to ship out, they asked me to come over to the their house and we got roaring drunk! And they gave me their most prized possession, a bottle of Johnny Red Walker. This was their expression of their feeling towards me, and I never forgot that moment, how close we had become through this journey.

War's End

In August, when we dropped the A-bomb, a lot of people now talk about what a terrible thing it was. To this day, I never regretted my feeling; I felt it was the right thing to do. And from a very personal perspective, I felt that was the thing that saved me! There wasn't overt cheering or anything. I know from the people that I was with, all of us were relieved.

In 1946, we landed in Camp Killmore in New Jersey, and the thing I remember the most was that huge steak that they served! That's all we ever talked about was steak and potatoes because we were getting K-rations – sometimes not even that – and the food was never very good.

It was a little bit of adjustment being back home. There were nights when I would wake up and I had nightmares, and I'd be just wet with sweat, because I'm still reliving some of those times of the fighting, because there were some real bad times. One time we had a real bad fire fight, and so the captain said, "Sgt. Chin, why don't you go with the grave detail and identify our people." And that was a terrible thing to have to do because you know it's pretty gruesome. People were chopped up. I was literally ill from that experience. I was just depressed by it all, but they don't give you much time for your own sorrows and the next thing you know you're already moving again to another attack. So there was a certain sense of desperation. You wonder when this thing is going to be

Ark G. Chin (left) and his father, Jang Teung Chin, 1943.
—Courtesy of Ark G. Chin.

over, because it was just an existence from one day to another. You see guys get hurt around you and once and awhile you have to think about it and then you try to put it out of your mind, otherwise you can't function.

In America after the war, there was still a certain amount of racial prejudice. For instance in my dad's restaurant, one time this guy was drunk. So he says, "You damn chinks. I fought for my country, I fought in the Marine Corps." I said, "So what! I fought in the 100th Infantry Division!" Didn't make any difference to him. He still had that redneck approach.

Interviewed by Pei Pei Sung.

Henry Yuen CHIN

World War II, Korean War and Vietnam War
Army, Combat Infantry and Intelligence Corps, 1944-1973
Sergeant 1st Class, Specialist-7

The Department of Defense sent a letter from the President of the United States – a rubber stamp signature, but nevertheless, it's sent directly to you – that the country needs to call on you. I grew up with the military so it never did bother me one way or another. Just another day. I could read a comic book and tell jokes and be happy in the frontline as well as in the rear, so it didn't bother me. Dad was in World War I a long, long time ago.

Boot camp seemed like a lot of fun. You got a chance to do a lot of macho things…like exercising and climbing the mountain, swinging on the high rope, a lot of things that you only saw in the movies. So we thought – not only me – a lot of fellows in those days thought, "Here's a chance…to grow up." I was just a happy kid in those days and I wasn't a career man or anything. Just do what they tell me to do.

By the time I finished school and basic training and all that, by the time they sent me to the war, the war was only two, three months from getting over. I didn't get to the Philippines until late May 1945 and the war ended in September. They just kept us at headquarters for combat support in Yokohama.

I mixed with the civilians. We tried to be friendly with them. Every side,

Combat is never glory. It's a serious job and somebody has to do it. Do it as honorably and as best you can…I hate war.

both sides in the war got their own propaganda…except we don't use "propaganda"; we use "truth." Your enemy uses the propaganda. And so we had to demonstrate that we meant to be friends. It's not the Japanese people's fault. It's just like in Europe too; it's not the German people's fault. They were the victim; they had no choice. If they didn't fight for their country when they're ordered to – just like our country – then they were mocked as a traitor.

After the war and all that excitement…I went to California to look for a job. Twelve, 13 million GIs came home and the war effort in the United States was all closed, the shipyard, Boeing, places they made guns, the places they made bombs. And then when those…closed, people were laid off. So I went to California, looked for work, and didn't do too good down there. I tried the farming. I tried the restaurants – Italian restaurants, Chinese restaurant, Japanese sukiyaki restaurant. And I wasn't that good of a cook.

Then I went to a tavern, had a few beers now and then, and talked to a guy who was drafted in there. The military was looking for ex-servicemen because they needed sergeants desperately to train the new draftee. And since I was already a paratrooper at that time, I volunteered for a different school. I was growing up fast, and I knew I needed some education and trade school at least. I didn't intend to stay in, but I could use the GI Bill and do something else. After I re-enlisted in 1948, the Korean War started in 1950, so I was caught on that one.

I was sent over there in reconnaissance unit and, at first, I was in the kitchen. I figured it would be the safest way, but not in the reconnaissance armor unit. You went right to the front line with them. They were killing our tankers like flies…so my company commander taught me how to drive a tank in two hours and I was a tank driver. Then I became a professional soldier, without thinking or realizing it.

Combat is never glory. It's a hell hole. It's a lot of pain and a lot of screaming before they die. The lucky one, I always believe, is the nuclear war casualty — poof; you go up into smoke. You don't have time to worry, to be scared or hurt or feel the pain. But some of us were not that lucky. And it's not lucky when you witness some of those casualties in combat. It's not glory. It's a serious job, and somebody has to do it. Do it as honorably, as best you can. You're not doing anything wrong because they are your enemy of your country. And you always find somebody on the wrong end of your sight on your rifle, but you got no choice. You have to survive.

Maybe, with God's help, we can stay away from war. I don't think I'm going to see that in my lifetime, but let's hope we can achieve that. War is not a beautiful glory. It's a horrible way to die, and that could be our own children dying and children's children. So before we decide to fight a war, we better make up our mind that we're going to win it. And don't fight at all. I hate war.

Interviewed by Pei Pei Sung.

—Courtesy of Henry Yuen Chin, 1967.

William "J.B." CHIN

World War II
Army, 121st Regiment, 8th Infantry Division, 1943-1945
Corporal

I was just like a dumb high school kid. I wasn't aware of anything. It never occurred to me to be afraid [of being drafted into the military]. I mean it's something we had to do and that was it. I guess I was drafted in the Army. I had no choice — Air Force or anything like that. It was just Army. And then — my parents don't know it — but I was getting bored and they went around camp asking for volunteers and I volunteered for overseas duty and that's how I ended up in Ireland with the 8th Infantry Division. That's why I've never volunteered for anything after.

This is war

One July 4, 1944, when we went ashore on Omaha Beach in Normandy, France, for one thing, you've never seen a dead body before. There were some of them floating in the water and lying on the beach. We were marched up to a hillside, and they told us we'd better start digging a trench, and that no, we don't have to worry. Pretty soon you hear some shells come over, then everyone starts digging a trench. Well, I guess, this is war. You're going to have to try and survive. I'm a fatalist. Whatever's going to happen is going to happen. So, I thought to myself, "If I'm going to get shot, I'm going to get shot."

Later, as prisoners of war, we were herded and locked into box cars called "forties and eights," as in 40 men or eight horses.

After Normandy, our division moved on to General Patton's breakthrough at St. Lo, then headed toward St. Malo and Brest in France then shifted towards Luxembourg, Belgium, and the Rhineland-Jurtgen Forest. On Nov. 30, 1944, we were out on patrol. I think there were 11 people. We were going down this ravine; we were supposed to patrol and look for enemy. Next minute we knew, there was gunfire. Germans had opened machine gunfire. I think they shot the radioman, and I think they shot the last guy at the end. We just laid there for awhile. Nobody made a sound. Nothing moved, because we didn't know what was going to happen. And, all of a sudden, the German popped out and said, "Surrender or I shoot." Everybody just dropped their guns and surrendered. The radio man who was wounded, we had to carry him on a door or board until he died. He died on the road.

The Germans marched us a little while until we got to a little house, and some German officer interrogated us. All we gave him was our rank and our serial number. I was scared and wondering what's going to happen. I said, "This. . .is going to be it." Later, we were herded and locked into box cars called "forties and eights," as in 40 men or eight horses. We departed from Flammershiem with stops at Düsseldorf, Bonn, Lumburg, Mulburg and arrived at Stalag IV-F in Leipzig, Germany after more than three weeks in transit. We were often strafed by American planes — mostly the locomotive would be hit — and then our train would sit idle 'til another locomotive was located. Those were times I thought of my parents, my family, my fiancee. I was remembering what they looked like and what they'd done for me and all that. I'm not very much of a church person, but I prayed silently.

I remember Stalag IV-F was a huge camp. They had barbed wires around there. In fact, I don't remember how I slept there. There was a lot of prisoners in there. The guards were kind of older men; they're not the young diehards. They were probably more compassionate than if they were regular SS troopers. They didn't treat you roughly. They didn't go out and abuse you. They're the guards and we're the prisoners, and you do whatever they ask you and then there's no fuss. We were fed rutabaga soup and dark German bread twice a day. On rare occasions, we got a small piece of horse meat.

On May 7, 1945, the Germans took us to the American lines, probably to gain favor since they kind of liberated some American prisoners of war. It was early in the morning and we were really happy. We were going to get home free! I left for the U.S. June 5, 1945 and arrived June 12th.

[Back in the United States], well, it was a lot different from prison camp and a lot different from Army life where sometimes you have to sleep out in the cold in a tent and all that. You come home, you get a nice warm bed and central heating and central plumbing.

The war changed me. Don't volunteer for anything! I became more reserved and less outgoing. I never go camping outdoors. You realize how precious your time on earth is. Here today, gone tomorrow. I remember there was a replacement kid that came up, and he was there for a few hours – he was gone. I found out that he had been shot the first time he went into battle. The only thing I could think of was, "This is the real thing." It's not fake anymore, not cops and robbers like when you play with kids. You used to shoot, "Bang-bang, you're dead." Now you can get shot and killed.

Interviewed by Lily Eng and David Elliott.

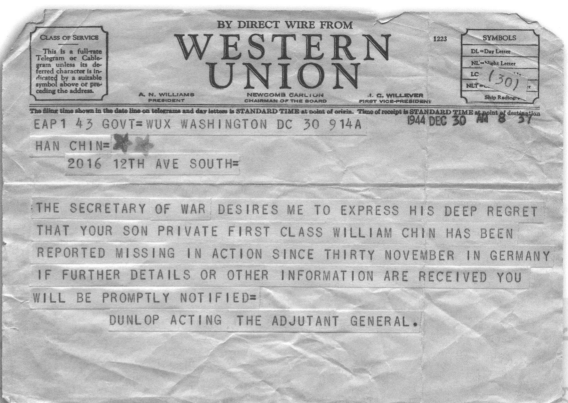

—*Artifacts courtesy of Dr. William "J.B." Chin*

Ron CHINN

Vietnam War
Army Ranger, 1967-1969
Captain

I never gave the military any thought – at all. In high school graduation year, when guys are going down to take the physical, I didn't make it to the physical. I went to a big party out in Maple Valley [Wash.] the day of the physical. I just thought it would blow over and never affect any of us.

There wasn't that much protesting going on then, but a lot of people thought that it wasn't our job to get involved and I kind of agreed with them.

{The summer he was inducted, Ron had left Seattle to work in Wenatchee with his father.} A postman came in with two FBI agents and asked Fey Dunmore, the manager who was standing right next to me at the cash register, if she knew where there was a Ronald H. Chinn. And I told them I was. They told me who they were and they had sent a draft notice to my home in Seattle and it was returned. They asked me to open the letter that they had. After I read it, they said, "Well, you have to come with us now." I didn't even get to go say goodbye to my dad.

It was quite a shock. The biggest shock…was when they said, "A through L, Army and L through Z, Marine Corps." Last name would've been Woo, I'd have been in the Marines. I thought about that on the train ride because my real family name is Woo. I could have told the FBI and the post inspector or whoever that guy was that

They were never going to be welcomed wherever they go. This is 1970, nobody wants them. Nobody wants me.

I wasn't Ronald Chinn. I was Woo Bouc Thin…that is my Chinese name. I could, but why get out of it? By the time I got to Tacoma [Wash.], I'd just come to terms with myself. Hey, okay, I'm in the Army. I'm stuck for two years. I just figured it would just blow over.

[During basic training, instructors] constantly picked on me because I was Oriental. Most of the drill instructors had already been to Vietnam. But I know why now that they were like that, but back then I didn't understand. They constantly called me a gook. My name wasn't Pvt. Chinn; it was gook. Another one could be Pvt. Swanson and I'd be Pvt. Gook. [Instructors] wanted to me to wash out of Officer Candidate School. They thought that no gook should lead their men to combat. I was always treated that way; they never let up.

When I got to Vietnam, I was with 14 other enlisted men. A big monster of a Black major came out of the long hooch, which was a headquarter. He told us immediately that he was executive officer of MacV compound. Then he looked down the line and saw me. I was at the end of the line because I was the only officer in the group. Then he started yelling real loud and he called our command sergeant out and demanded him to tell him why there was a gook in his formation. He kept yelling and screaming and telling some to "lock and load. Shoot the son of a bitch. He cannot be on our base; this is a maximum security base." He kept yelling that over and over. I didn't know what to make of that guy, but when he cooled off, the command sergeant major took me away. Then later they told me he was going to put me in a bunker down by the air field. They would segregate me and my team from the rest of the compound. I stayed in the bunker in between missions. I knew that if I got anywhere near headquarters, I was going to waste that executive officer. I remember telling a lot of people "Hey, what are they going to do? Send me to Vietnam?" That was a very old saying over there. What can they do, send us here? It can't be any worse.

The first mission, I lost the captain and one other guy that night. The intelligence said that there might or might not be any enemy up there… So we split the team in half. There were only six of us. Three went on one side. Three of us went around the back. And we were just going to go up to the beginning of the enemy's perimeter – if they had one – and just sense how many people they had up in that area. And then hug the perimeter and watch them throughout the day. That night, we would just slip off the hill and meet up down below. But something happened. I don't know why they started shooting. Somebody started shooting…and the three on the other side, the captain and the sergeant were both killed instantly and the other one was shot in the shoulder and in the hip.

When the shooting stopped, the three of us backed up as far as we could and went around and started going back down the other side of the hill, which wasn't going to receive any direct fire. So we went back up and found them.

We got into a few skirmishes going across the valley [back to the fire base] but we made it over there. Each one of us had to carry somebody. And it's very hard to carry somebody and fight – especially when I was carrying the sergeant who was killed. He was very heavy and dead weight and it was very hot, so it was very difficult to move around 'cause every 100 feet or so, there's a booby trap. Remember we were in Vietnam, so there's the luxury and comforts of booby traps and snakes and all the normal things.

When I got hit in the hip up on fifth or sixth mission and everyone else got hit too, we had no team. We were all in hospitals. They sent me home to the United States for seven days leave. When I got off the plane at McChord [Air Force Base in Washington], a big brown sack came flying over the fence and I watched it coming down. It just splattered right in front of me and it was all full of crap – human crap. I wondered what was that for and I asked an airman. Well, Jane Fonda and some Indians were on the other side of the fence protesting the war in Vietnam. Well this is not home. So I turned around and got back on the plane and told them I was with MacV and told them I was on a CIA assignment and I wanted to go back. I was home probably an hour or an hour and a half, whatever time it took them to unload the plane, refuel and leave. I never wanted to come back to this country even if they forced me to. After two-and-a-half years in Vietnam, it didn't seem like my home anymore.

I know people who were in my team…and were proud of themselves. They wanted to go home and show their families their uniforms and the ribbons they got. I knew some guys on the plane were talking, wondering where can they get boot polish. They wanted to shine their boots a little more. I kept thinking to myself: "They're never going to be welcomed wherever they go. This is 1970, nobody wants them. Nobody wants me."

Interviewed by Ken Mochizuki and Chanh Norsouvanh.

Teresita Iriarte COALSON

Vietnam War
Women's Army Corps, Military Intelligence, 1968-1991
Master Sergeant, E-8

Growing up in Guam, I realized that even then, the military had a lot of impact in my life. The bombs that came out of Guam to Vietnam – I remember, as a young girl, seeing the bombs transported from the southern end of the island, where they were put together.

Many of my young friends never thought not to enlist. For them, it was a badge of courage, a sign of adulthood to go into the military. I had met a young soldier about the same time. When he was in Vietnam, he had been injured and he had to return. It was probably first love, but he died. And about the same time, I had lost several other friends. I think then that I felt the need to do something for my country.

I think in that time, it was okay to go to war; we were doing it for a cause. Even seeing the riots, those people who were against Vietnam War burning flags, we were so patriotic towards America, the land of the free…that it was a real dishonor… that was given to the country by those demonstrators. So my view of war was that what we were doing was an honorable thing. I had this patriotic fervor. I was going to do for God and country, and I did it.

Initially, I was going in the Air Force. At the recruiting office one day… I had to have pictures taken in local dress…I said, "What is the picture all

I had this patriotic fervor. I was going to do this for God and country, and I did it.

about?" And they told me that they had sent the pictures to the Air Force office in Washington, D.C., and they had decided that I could go work in the Pentagon. I was going to be a stenographer. I asked, "How come I got this assignment?" I don't know why it just struck me wrong. They said, "Well, 'cause you look so pretty in your pictures." I said, "This is stupid. What if I looked ugly in my pictures? Where would I go?" So I told the recruiter for the Air Force that I'm not going to the Air Force. And the Army recruiter said, "You'll be the first Chamorro lady to be in Military Intelligence." You can be ugly and be in Military Intelligence. So I figured fine. I'll go and be in the Army and go to Military Intelligence.

I ended up becoming an assistant instructor and a demonstrator. I played parts in exercises the schools ran in various classes. I would play the part of a Vietnamese person, or a VC (Vietcong) person, a barmaid or a wife. When I first got approached to do this, I was a bit hesitant because I knew what the exercises were about and that not many females were involved in the unit, but they needed the females to play the parts; it was a duty type thing and that's exactly how they put it and that's exactly how I saw it. My first part was very simple and it was that of a wheat farmer's wife. As the time went on and I took on more parts, then the parts got a little more difficult because they involved really quick thinking on your feet, and they also involved parts of the enemy.

There was an incident with an individual who was supposed to interrogate me. There were usually monitors there, especially when there's a female involved, but my monitor had stepped out to get a cigarette. And hindsight being what it is, I think the man doing the interrogation was exhausted. He was Special Forces. Most of them had been to

Vietnam two or three times…Before I could say anything, he had just picked me up and wanted to ask me questions and just basically threw me because he was having a flashback. In my mind I was thinking, "Geneva Conventions! Geneva Conventions!" I really didn't have a chance to get it out. I hit the board; he hit me against it pretty hard. And the monitor came in and everything ceased at that time. That memory kind of rankles in my mind. Thinking about it, I hold no animosity towards the individual, but it was frightening – more now than I think it was then. I had bruises, but because of the way it happened and where we were at, it was kind of expected even though it was unexpected. I basically put myself together and took a time out from the exercise and then went back in.

I think by my accepting it as a norm, there was really no room to complain. Whatever came my way, I would take. Every other soldier or sailor was probably facing the same difficulty. Probably, that was a good survival technique.

Dealing with racism and sexism

I was assigned to Fort Hollibird, Md. When I walked to the general subject session, I heard the man who was about to become my boss say, "We need someone to come in and serve as an assistant instructor to this place. I can handle anybody, just as long as it's not one of them women, and as long as it's not an Islander." And he turned around and it was me. Right from the get go, I had in the back of my mind that I really had to serve as a role model.

I had several incidents where not accepting a date, you were called a lesbian or a dyke. If you accepted a date with the concept that it was just a date, they would think, "You're a woman in the military, what are you there for?" As I went up higher in the ranks, then I had to deal with more insidious, more covert type of sexual harassment. This was where someone pats you on the arm and you politely say, "That doesn't happen." And they question you and make statements like, "What are you talking about, that was just a friendly gesture." They make you want to question your sanity sometimes or your reasoning or your logic. This is where you bring it up to the chain of commands and their comeback is: "First of all, it is just a guy thing, and if you didn't want it you wouldn't be there." Or [the commanders would say], "You just imagined it, it didn't happen."

I retired from the military in 1991. I realized that I was having difficulty sleeping. Found myself getting violently ill, severe headaches, throwing up on the way to classes. I realized that something was not right. I started thinking about it and then one day it hit me…the sexual harassment issues hit the fan: Command

sergeant major of the Army, the Aberdeen Proving Grounds [sexual harassment cases involving military personnel during the 1990s. One day driving down the road…I found myself thinking that I could just press that accelerator and just run that car into the wall. Ended up me coming home and making a call to the vet's

Retired Master Sergeant Coalson (third row, second from left) in Women's Army Corps, 1968. –Courtesy of Teresita Iriarte Coalson.

center. I couldn't even talk, just sobbed my whole way through. I…found myself really looking at an individual who was ready to explode.

The outcome of the sexual harassment trial was that Command Sgt. Maj. McKinney [who pressed charges against her male colleagues] was labeled a slut, a liar by the defense. And I think that was the match to the stick of dynamite. It was the combination of all the things that I've seen. I found myself thinking… I know that I'm not the only one who suffered to try to make a change, to try to make it better. And this is happening to a sergeant major? I actually broke down and cried…and so it was just like a flood of tears for all the things that women have suffered. And it just seemed like it was the time to stop. I guess when one has suffered so much for something that they look at it as something noble, a noble cause, a calling, it was just too much.

Interviewed by Ken Mochizuki and Pei Pei Sung.

Gene del ROSARIO

World War II
Navy, USS Nassau, 1942-1945
2nd Class (D), V-6 Captain

One morning in March 1942, I went out to Mary's Café, a Filipino restaurant [in Seattle's International District]. There was a White guy and a Chinese recruiter. One of them said, "Hey, you guys. Don't you know that you can already get in the Navy?" I was going to wait for my draft, but I went to my draft board because I like to go in the service right away. The recruiter said, "If you want to come in the Navy, we can fix that for you so you can get in right away." And that's what I did.

My thing is to avenge Bataan, the fall of Bataan, Philippines. I didn't want to sit down here and let the fight do it for me. I was happy to join any branch of service, but it just so happened that the Navy came and got me first. I just was so mad that the Japanese sneak attack on Pearl Harbor and the Philippines at that time. I really liked to be in the front line. I wanted to fight. That's all there was to it. I didn't even think of dying. I was not afraid during the war, I was not afraid of dying. I just wanted to go fight and see what I could do.

I was a captain gunner during combat, but usually, I was a steward. I was the one in charge of the wardroom, the dining room. I inspected how other stewards fixed the beds of the officers. That's the one good thing about the Navy: Even if you are in the combat zone, you got a nice bed. You got a spring bed, mattress, bed sheets, not like in the Army where you dig your fox hole and stay in there even if it's raining.

As long as we're not in the combat zone, we ate good food. Breakfast is about six o'clock to eight and then lunch time. If we're not in the combat zone, you eat anytime. If you are hungry, you just go and eat your lunch. But when you are in the combat zone, that's it. But if you were not, you ate good food. We even got steak. Then lunch, from 11 to one o'clock. Then in the evening, from six o'clock in the evening to almost eight o'clock for dinner. [In between meals], we played volleyball, threw baseball. Sometimes we got three courts: one in the fantail, one in the mid-section of the aircraft carrier and then one in the aft. We played mostly volleyball during the day, but at night, well, whatever. I wrote letters. I would go up the flight deck, especially when it's moonlight, then I could think lots. I could make story or poem. Inside, you played cards until lights out. Then, we just talked to each other, told stories in our quarters.

One time we were attacked when we were in the Gilbert Islands. The watchman didn't see the Japanese plane in the radar. You should see the blood – the bullet from the plane that attacked us went through the flight deck through the hanger deck. There were quite a few casualties because it was lunch time and a lot of us were just lining up to get ice cream. That's the time I had seen a lot of blood. I said, "That's blood flowing in there? Oh my God." That's all I could say. Then somebody told me, "Your friend got hit." "This is war," I said to myself, "This is war. If it's your time, you're going to go."

Filipino veterans who enlisted from the United States are all forgotten. Just like they have the 1st Filipino Infantry and the 2nd Filipino Infantry [U.S. regiments during World War II] and the people who joined the Navy, Coast Guard, Air Force, things like that, we are just forgotten. My ship participated in five major battles, from the retaking of Attu Islands to Australia and the liberation of the Philippines. We paved the way for Gen. Douglas MacArthur's return to the Philippines. Even our own people, they forget us already. We Filipinos who served in the U.S. Armed Forces are veterans, but forgotten veterans.

I was happy to join any branch of the service. I was just so mad that the Japanese sneak an attack on Pearl Harbor and the Philippines at the same time.

Interviewed by Lily Eng and Susan Almachar.

Eddie N. DETERA

Vietnam War
Navy, 1963-1984
E-6

The only impression of the U.S. military I had was from these people we heard were joining the Navy. Also, I remember when you were graduating from high school or elementary school, and you got this picture book. A lot of kids wrote, "What do you want to be in life?" and a lot of them wanted to be in the U.S. Navy. Well, it was very hard to join the Navy in the Philippines…'cause you had to go to a lot of competitions. I was just lucky enough to have a chance to take the test. Maybe during that week, 80 of our people took the test and after that, they scheduled you for a physical, interview and all this stuff only for the people who passed. And I still remember that of 80 applicants, only about two of us made it.

At last, I got to see the states. The only time I saw the states was in a color picture or magazine and in the movies. We were flown to the U.S. around Dec. 31st. And in my dream, going from a tropical climate like the Philippines, so warm even December months, and then being flown to San Francisco where it's so cold. Oh boy! And that was the first time I'd been in that kind of weather.

When we started training in San Diego, that's when we had a chance to be with this group of Americans and some Colored guys. The first time I saw White people, they were already all shaven like us too. When they're in the training they shave their hair off. I couldn't tell the difference; they were all the same. Likewise too for them; they could not tell who's who among the Filipinos…but after a while, they would say the name and remember the faces.

When we joined the Navy in the Philippines, we signed something, like that's the kind of job we're going to have in the Navy. And also, we signed one of the forms that states we don't intend to be American citizen. Those days all the recruitment for stewards and cooks were the Asians, or the Filipinos and the Blacks. Our supervisors were Black or Filipinos. I didn't see any White people supervising us.

During my 20 years, I did experience discrimination. A few people wouldn't like your color. I worked for this White American and we were in the same section. He was the supervisor. He didn't like that I made advancements kind of fast. Before he assigned those White Americans any duties, he had to get me first. Then those White Americans who we were on the ship, they would just be staying in the ship, just playing whatever, but I'd be out there working. That's when I realized that I was not being treated right. There was this branch; if you're not being handled right, you could go and complain. I did and I found out that these people knew each other so whenever you made a complaint, nothing happens. But there were a lot of White Americans who I worked for, and they're really nice. They treated you like everybody else, treated you like a first class American.

My first ship, I kind of liked it —

Some of my friends, after 20 years, they retire only E-3. In 10 years, I was already E-6! I could have gone on to be an officer.

months, and then being flown to San Francisco where it's so cold. Oh boy! And that was the first time I'd been in that kind of weather.

working and learning what to do…then you would learn the shortcuts. The first time, I was in a boarder ship and I didn't know about being seasick and when the big waves hit, I said, "I don't like being here." But what could you do, you were already there. The first few days I was feeling very sick and always throwing up. But after a week or so, I got kind of used to it.

Then I didn't like the job…'cause it was like being a maid. But when we hit port, we got liberty time. That was the best part for me. When you hit port, you got a little money that you can spend, go around. But after that, same routine: get up early, set the table for officers. After breakfast, we would clean again then dress up in the blue uniforms for working the state building, picking up laundry, even making up their beds, taking it to the laundry. I'd be assigned to...20 state rooms. In one state room, there were about three, four officers. I had to take care of all those and clean it up, then come lunch time, be ready to set the table, serve them again. And after, get dressed up again and continue working in the state room, laundry and all that. Then come dinner time, get dressed again in new whites, set the table, serve them, and clean it up. After work, then we would get a break, then that's when we rest. That's a long day!

I was a steward for five years until I was able to switch rate. I was a hydraulic mechanic for nine years until I switched rate again to become an aviation storekeeper. I did that until I retired.

I can still remember during those times we were with the Vietnam mortars. Our ship also fired guns over in Vietnam and I was assigned to be a lookout. You would watch the war to see if there's anything not ordinary going on. Maybe there were some people trying to sabotage the ship. I didn't really think about war that much. My job was just to work for this officer. We were not exposed out there like these people really manning the guns. And it wasn't like being really in war, because our involvement was really just cooking.

The ship was hit. I only found that out when I was trying to put in my record all the medals that I was entitled to. Military officials told me, "You're also entitled for this Navy Comet Medal because of that time the ship was hit." I'd been there all that time and I didn't know about it. Maybe the high ranking officers knew what went on but never did tell the people who we were hit.

I got my citizenship, I think, in 1970. Just like the rest of those Filipinos ahead of me, I learned from them how you apply and what kind of questions they asked you. Like I said before, we signed a form that said we don't intend to be an American citizen. After 1963, there was a change. Maybe a change was made, like they have this thing called shipping over. I signed for six years. After six years, if you want to go for another ten, that's what they call a shipping over. And something regarding shipping over that you could be qualified to apply for American citizenship, and that's what I did.

I don't really know why I did become a citizen. Those other Filipinos are doing it, so why not? So I went, didn't really think that much, but I didn't even think of going anywhere. I was thinking of just staying in the Navy for 20 years. Because after the first time I said to myself, "I'm just going to stay here." That's how I can support my family. The Navy was being very good to me. I got free hospital care. I decided to stay for more than 20 years, about 21 years. If I didn't like it, I would not just stay 20 years with the military. And still, like now, I'm enjoying the benefits that I'm getting from it. I wouldn't say it's a successful career, but it's been a career. For people that have really made it a career, they went high and achieved what they want to achieve. I didn't achieve really what I wanted to achieve.

Interviewed by Eydie Detera and Pei Pei Sung.

–Courtesy Eddie N. Detera, circa 1970.

Mike HIGASHI

Vietnam War
Army, 172nd Preventive Medicine Company, 1967-1970
Specialist-5

My father is a World War II Nisei [second generation Japanese American] veteran. He served in the Pacific. He was with Military Intelligence Service and he was a combat interrogator. My mother, she was sent to [internment] camp, but she was able to get out of camp because she was able to find a job opportunity in Chicago.

It was not unusual for MIS (Military Intelligence Service) Nisei veterans not to talk about their service when I was growing up back in the '60s. The reason why is because their job was top secret, and apparently, it was termed confidential for the longest time even in peace time.

I graduated in 1966, and then I went to the University of Washington. This was during the draft, during the war in Vietnam, and I enlisted after my first year at the U because my grades weren't very good. By enlisting, I was able to choose basically what my job could be. I went down to the enlistment office, and then I looked to see what there was. I was interested in medical corps of some type, and so I went down the list, and I found something that I liked, preventive medicine. I signed up for a three year term and that's how I started. I guess part of it was self-survival. Rather than just going in and being infantry, combat

infantry or armor or things like that, I wanted a duty where I could learn something so that when I got out, it could help me out as far as what I wanted to do. If I was still interested in medicine, at least it would kind of help me. And I really didn't want to be a medic because that's pretty rough.

During basic training, I was treated just as badly as everybody else. In my mind, there was no regard to race or color. We all had to do our job and we all had the training to go through. I was not given any special treatment nor was I picked on.

When you're a young person and you're not even 21, you just kind of take each day at a time. I just never thought about war…Maybe I thought it was exciting.

When you're a young person and you're not even 21, you just kind of take each day at a time. You're in the service for a number of years, so basically you just do what you're told and you do your job, and just let the day go by. I just never thought about war. Maybe I thought it was exciting.

Preventive medicine is a support unit, and we help take care of the troops. And so we basically had our own unit, and we were at what's called a base camp which is relatively nice. It's out in the field. We had buildings to stay in, like hooches made out of wood and with corrugated steel roofs. We weren't living in tents. We were living in something structured. So then we had mess halls where we could go, and then we had jeeps and vehicles and everything else. We were to train the non-commissioned officers about basic hygiene and taking care of…malaria; taking care of sewage and latrines, how to make them, how to maintain them; doing mess hall inspections, making sure that the food was kept at proper temperatures.

On camp, in our units, Vietnamese civilians did menial things, like cleaning up the hooches where we stayed, or…sand bagging. The ones who were there on a regular basis, we had nicknames for them and they were very friendly. If you didn't know a Vietnamese and they were working inside the compound, then they were either going to be a mama-san or a papa-san. That's a carry over from World War II. It was a lot more polite to use that word – mama-san or papa-san – than it is to say, gook, slope, chink. You heard those slurs all the time. I didn't use those terms because it could have easily been used on me.

When men got together and you had a few drinks…it was not unusual to kid around. And I remember instances where my friends…would say, "Hey, gook, get me another beer." And so in that context, there was a familiarity that friends get when they think they're being cute. Well, you just didn't make a big deal about it, but you didn't have to like it either. But you kind of go along with the flow because that's the atmosphere that's over there. Life is hard enough.

Whenever we went off base, I remember we always had our M-16 because you never knew what was going to happen. But wherever I was, it was relatively safe. I was always with a large enough number. It'd be kind of risky to go off base by yourself, so you just kind of went with a buddy system, at least two of you guys. I remember being in South Vietnam, and I was really dark. It was not unusual for me to walk around and get a Black Power salute from a Black GI going down in a truck or something.

Once you're in a war zone and you're in the whole atmosphere, it's the same thing day in and day out. It can actually get kind of boring. But you're out there, you know a war is going on. You can see the planes. You can hear the bombs. You can feel the ground shake. And you see prisoners of war. You know it's happening, but you're so engulfed in it that basically it's just one day after another.

Near the tail end of the war, we were of the same mind that it was not working out, that we really should go home, and that there was a lot of waste of men. When I went back to Fort Lewis [in March 1970], I knew that I did not really want to wear my uniform. It was enough of a stigma to be a veteran at that time. You just wanted to slip in really quietly. When I got home, I was just tired. I just wanted to rest and relax.

It's funny being a veteran; you saw both sides. One side you wanted to support the guys who were in Vietnam because you already were there and you knew that you really didn't choose to be there, but you're there. But on the other hand, you realized that the ones who were protesting were also shortening the war. And so by protesting they were also doing their part. And if they really felt strongly about it, well then you had to admire them for doing it. So it's kind of with mixed emotions that a veteran will see a protest. There may have been some veterans that did, but for the most part, I think most of us just wanted to get on with our lives. We had already done our duty. We had already served our time and we just wanted to move on.

[Regarding Japanese American veterans of World War II], that's tremendous to have the whole society look at you as an enemy. But I have to give them credit for having the courage to volunteer, even under an unjust situation, to fight for our country that kept their families behind barbed wire, and to go out and to perform at the level that they performed at – it's unbelievable. What they did allowed Japanese Americans like myself to be able to be a serviceman and not have stigma associated with me. They served so well that it's a legacy that we should all be proud of and that we should all respect.

Interviewed by Pei Pei Sung.

Paul HOSODA

World War II and Korean War
Army, 442nd Regimental Combat Team, 1943-1946
Counter Intelligence Corps, 1950-1968
Chief Warrant Officer, Grade 4

[When the Japanese bombed Pearl Harbor], I was a 17-year-old freshman at the University of Utah. I was really shocked and concerned. I think I was more concerned about what the people would do about those of Japanese ancestry who were residing in our area. I felt that one of the things that I should do is volunteer for service. I attempted to join the service – Marines, Navy, Air Force – none of them would touch us, and the Army wouldn't. We had some very good friends in St. Anthony City [Idaho] – the mayor, sheriff, the school superintendent and all these prominent business people who were family friends – so I talked to some of them and I tried to get drafted, but all Japanese Americans were classified 4C Enemy Alien and we couldn't do anything then.

I attended a cooking school and then I started working as a cook. Around early spring 1943, the military mentioned that they were forming an all Japanese American unit [the 442nd Regimental Combat Team (RCT)] and that we could volunteer for that. I contacted my draft board so they called me up by the draft and sent me in.

[After training, the battalion sailed to Europe.] We docked in Italy. I

It seemed we were always told to dig foxholes in certain areas and then no sooner were we settled when we would be told to prepare to move out.

was assigned to be the Browning Automatic Rifleman. The rifle weighed over 20 pounds. Being just a private, I didn't know too much about what we were doing or why we were moving to another position. It seemed we were always told to dig foxholes in certain areas and then no sooner were we settled when we would be told to prepare to move out.

Our first exposure to enemy fire was when the RCT was given our first order to seek and attack the enemy. Our company was advanced to behind the other two lead companies, but because of poor communication, our company didn't know that the attack was delayed an hour. We just…marched up in there. As soon as we were fired upon, we dispersed like we were told to do. Eventually, those who were able regrouped behind some small hills. Later on, we heard this was the Battle of Belvedar, in which the 100th Battalion went around, made a sweep to the side and came in on the side on the enemy. The next thing we knew, we were marching in on the hill that they had captured and there were these guys from the 100th Battalion riding around on bicycles and driving the German jeeps, having a good time like school kids with a new toy. It was kind of cute to see that.

After receiving my discharge from the Army in 1946, I stayed in the reserves. They had a national guard unit in Idaho and some of my friends and I joined that…because the guard units were more active. I got myself a promotion from corporal all the way up to first sergeant. In 1950, our national guard unit was activated for the Korean War. Our primary mission was to build roads, bridges and to make it easy for the troops and supplies to be transported to the front lines.

From my own observations and from conversations with fellow Japanese Americans serving in Korea, the exploits and fame of the 442nd was a blessing for some and a handicap for others. When they went in the service into Korea, they followed after the regiment 442, the most decorated unit in U.S. history. Some high-ranking officers who knew about the record of the 442nd expected the Japanese Americans serving under them to perform in the same manner. Many of them probably felt gung-ho enough that they didn't want to smirch the record of the 442nd and so they would go all out and they took a lot of punishment themselves.

On the other hand, some Caucasian officers…would give Japanese Americans the opportunity for further advancement and everything, so many of the people who went to Korea came out as officers. During World War II, there were very few Japanese Americans commissioned as majors or higher; the majority were captains or lieutenants. It was gratifying to see that after that war and during the Korean War, there were those who received officer commissions as high as colonel. I felt that the door was opened for them to go up in the rank as they did because of what the 442nd regiment had done. I was able to retire as a chief warrant officer, grade four.

Many people in America don't know or appreciate what they've got. They've never been under bombardment. They've never had their food supply or fuel denied them. They've never been threatened by enemy troops. When I was in Europe, Japan or Korea, I'd look at the people, see how they suffered and abhorred war. You figure that the common people are not the ones who wanted this. It's always the politicians and businessmen who didn't want to lose enterprises and their opportunities. Those who didn't want to lose their privileges are the ones who are instigating all the problems that result in wars.

Interviewed by Pei Pei Sung and Geneva Witzleben.

Joseph A. KAMIKAWA

Korean War
Army Airborne, 187th Regimental Combat Team, 1951-1953
Staff Sergeant

One of my remembrances from Minidoka internment camp was the beautiful honor roll display they had in the front which listed all the names of the family members who had people in the armed services. Of course, my brother's name was on it so I was quite proud of it. He volunteered for military service right after Pearl Harbor. I kind of looked up to the men of the 442nd [Regimental Combat Team (RCT) of Japanese Americans] and what they were accomplishing. Every article I could find in *The Pacific Citizen* [the Japanese American Citizens League newspaper], the Minidoka papers, I looked up what they were doing as my heroes. They had quite an influence.

My brother shared some stories, but they weren't any combat stories. He shared stories about his relationship with other soldiers there, what they would do and what they found interesting when they were on leave and things like that. But combat is not a very pleasant subject to be talking about, especially if you lost friends.

As a youngster you really can't understand the total effect of what social impacts are going to be in the future. You kind of take it a day at a time. Everything was so uncertain at camp anyway. There was no question: The only country I knew was the United States. I wanted to do all I could to help our country. I volunteered for the service as soon as I turned 17. My mind was made up. When you're about 17 to 20, you figure you know a lot more than people give you credit for. You just think you know a lot about a lot of things. And out of that kind of blind ignorance, you do a lot of things you wouldn't do if you were fully informed. I wanted to be in the military. I wanted to get out. I wanted to travel. I wanted to have adventure. So I think those were the things that were really intriguing me and pulling me to the military.

The war was over when I volunteered in 1946. I figured I had to get training in military occupation, especially in something that I enjoyed. The only thing that I could think of honestly that I really enjoyed and wanted to know more about were cars. I was trained in automotive repair — this is with military vehicles. That took care of my first three years in the military. Then I decided I wanted something a little more exciting and that's when I volunteered for the paratroopers.

I recall one time in Military Operations School, I sat next to a staff sergeant who was so thin. I thought maybe he had tuberculosis or something because he was so thin. The instructor asked us each to get up and tell us a little background about where you're from and why you're in the service and what have you. And his name was Sgt. Johns and he was sitting next to me 'cause my name is Kamikawa and we sat alphabetically. Sgt. Johns stood up and said, "I was in the Bataan Death March. And I was a prisoner of the Japanese for something like 40 months." He wasted down to almost a skeleton as far as weight was concerned when he was finally released when World War II ended. It had to be probably around fall of '46 so it had been 18 months since he was out

I volunteered for the service as soon as I turned 17.
I wanted to be in the military. I wanted to get
out. I wanted to travel. I wanted to have adventure.

of prison and he was still quite thin. He said of the Japanese, "Those no good SOBs." I remember after he got through, he got a standing ovation. The whole class got up and cheered him and welcomed him back. Then I went ahead and said, "Some of you people have already called me Kamekaze so you know I'm Japanese, but I was born here. I am what we call Nisei. I am an American." I made it short and sweet and just said, "Nisei is American and I hope you can see it as such." And then I sat down. I think the positive twist of the whole story is that at the end of the eight weeks of automotive electrical training, Sgt. Johns and I became very close friends and we wished each other well on our assignments. That really shook me when he told his story. I would have been okay if there were four or five other people in between, but right after he sat down then I had to stand up and I had to address the fact of who I was. I was never ashamed of who I was, but at that point I'd rather have been quiet.

I was working as a physio-therapist. I thought I was pretty safe. All I had to do was sign up for a jump and I'd get jump pay, the rest of the time I was on the staff at the hospital. But then they got an order for a military specialist in physio-therapy for Tokyo General or Osaka because there was a lot of wounded. The Korean war had started. I went overseas approximately a year after the war started in Korea. But when I landed at Camp Drake, I was surprised to see my name on the bulletin board as a member of the 187th RCT. I wasn't going to be assigned to Osaka or Tokyo General because I had airborne training, paratrooper training and was just the person to fill one of the ranks of the casualties they suffered on their second drop.

We had a group of Christian GIs who took interest in other things. At the time I arrived in Japan, there were 33 children born to girls who were either raped or they were friends of the GIs. They had these 33 children in an orphanage sponsored by a church in Beppu. And one night, they had a terrible fire and my mother in-law approached me. She said, "Could you maybe ask somebody in the military base to help because 33 of these children are mixed blood children. We know that they need help and, especially after the fire, they need blankets. They need some money. Do you know anyone whom I can contact?" I had a personal friend, Kenneth O'Connell who was the original Red Cross Director. And then I approached other officers who I was very close to. They said, "Oh that sounds like a wonderful idea. Why don't you announce that and see how the GIs respond." I think on the first payday, they gave something like $10,000.

I had the luxury of taking care of the enemy. After U.S. soldiers took him back to the lines, they wanted to dress his wounds and pump him for all the information they could. And Capt. Miller said, "Kamikawa, go ahead and take care of him." So I cleaned his wound with peroxide, shaved around the wound and I said, "Okay now, Captain, he's ready for suture." He said, "No, I told you to take care of him. You suture. My last combat jump, two of our medical officers were wounded and were carried off the scene. And if the sergeants aren't prepared to take over, these guys are going to die." I knew how to use that little fishhook to suture a needle, but I never learned how to tie a suture knot so I tied a boy scout knot. I put five stitches in it and gave him a big shot of penicillin.

I never had people who thanked me for being a Korean War veteran until I went to Korea [for a 50th anniversary reunion]. There you see people about my age and they actually stop you — we had a little ribbon on us that said Korean War Veterans — and they would bow like the Japanese used to bow to the Emperor, a real low bow. And not for three seconds; in fact, you almost get uncomfortable. And you know they're doing it out of sincerity that at first I thought, is this staged? Us old paratroopers — here we're in our 70s, we're milder and we're different. You see some of these veterans and their eyes just well up in tears because for the first time, they're being thanked.

Interviewed by Carina A. del Rosario.

Jimmie KANAYA

World War II, Korean War and Vietnam War
Army Medical Dept., 442nd Regimental Combat Team, 1941-1974
Colonel

As a teenager, I was always fascinated with all the military branches. As soon as the draft started in 1940, I thought about volunteering to beat the draft. I tried the Marines and the Navy but they just looked at me and shook their heads. They suggested that I try the Army.

After basic training in the Army Air Corps, I was assigned to an Army General Hospital to drive the fire truck. On the first trial run, I forgot to double-clutch the gear and the truck came to a halt. All of the firemen hanging on to the side of the truck fell off! There went my career as a fireman.

After the Japanese bombed Pearl Harbor, about the middle of March, we were all gathered together and the commanding officer came down and talked to us Niseis [second generation Japanese Americans]. He said, "We've got to move you out." We had to leave the West Coast. They evacuated us inland and many of us ended up in Missouri.

I was put in charge of the Red Cross at the Station Hospital in Camp Crowder, Mo. Word got around that they were going to form an all-Nisei unit: the 442nd [Regimental Combat Team] at Camp Shelby, Miss. I told my first sergeant: "Let me know when that comes up because I want to go." Sure enough, I was on a three-day pass to Kansas City and when I came back, I was already promoted to first sergeant of this medical unit we were going to form in Camp Shelby. I had a

We hiked about 374 miles in the snow. Out of the 1,400 prisoners, about 1,000 of them dropped along the way.

cadre of 10 men to activate the medical detachment. That was quite an experience for me because during my very short tour in the Army, I didn't know what a first sergeant was supposed to do. Being in charge of all enlisted men, I had to relay orders from the officers. I wasn't older than the rest of them but I had the rank. It was hard; I developed hives and an excruciating sinus condition. One guy wanted my job – he was one rank below me – so I said, "I'll trade places with you." I took over this medical section in the 3rd Battalion...just before we went overseas. That cured my hives.

Captured by the Germans

During one mission in Europe, there were about three or four wounded lying in a house that we had to evacuate. We couldn't carry three or four litter cases with just the four of us medics so we stayed overnight, hoping for more help. During the evening, there were some more wounded. The next morning, we had to get ready to bring them back. There were about 35 or 40 German prisoners who were going to help us carry these patients back across the mountains through German territory. About halfway over the mountains, we were stopped by Germans. They wouldn't let us through. Next thing you know, the Germans came around and captured all of us. The German prisoners took the rifles...and they became the guards and we became the prisoners. Halfway back to the German lines, we heard a round of gunfire. There was a German non-commissioned officer who took my wristwatch when we were first captured. He came running back and he gave my wristwatch back to me. He thought we would be recaptured by our side. But then, after we finally got back to the secured German lines, he came back and took my watch again!

In the prisoner-of-war (POW) camp, called Oflag 64, we usually got enough water to drink, but we were always hungry. One of the doctors figured out the ration we got everyday…it was barely enough to keep a sick man alive in bed – about 700 calories a day. We were supposed to get one Red Cross box a week and there was about 12 pounds of food in it. After about the first month I was there, we didn't get any more Red Cross boxes. Everybody was losing weight.

Towards the end of the war – this was Jan. 21st of 1945 – Poland was being overrun by Russia so they moved 1,400 of us out of camp. In northern Poland, snow was on the ground. We didn't have winter boots or gloves so most of us got frostbite. I got sick towards the end. We were eating out of rusty cans and eating anything we could get a hold of. Every mile, we kept track of. We hiked about 374 miles in the snow. By the time the group reached the final POW camp, we ended up with about 400. Out of the original 1,400 prisoners, most of were overrun by the Russian Army or evacuated medically.

Escaping POW camp

On April 4, 1945, rumors were floating around that we were being moved to the Bavarian Alps and would be held as hostages. I made up my mind that I was going to escape. When the platoon I was in finally moved out and joined the column that afternoon, I noted the direction, bridge and anything that I could use as a landmark. Two hours after we left camp, we were strafed by our own planes. The whole column split to either side of the road. I was on the right hand side so I took off and ran about 100 yards. I hid in a depression in the ground that was covered with overhanging foliage. After about 10 minutes, the German guards came out and hollered, "Everybody back on the road." I just stayed there.

Just before it got dark, I crawled out to survey the situation. Before I did, I buried a Prince Albert tobacco can with a table knife, pictures and anything else that might incriminate me if I was caught. Nine years later, while stationed in Germany, I located the exact spot in the woods where I buried that can and I found it! The can had melted, rusted off, but the knife and spoon, some of the metal parts are still there. I still have that.

Since it was still semi-light, I was able to locate the railroad line and the bridge that I wanted to avoid. I stumbled down the bank about 100 yards before the bridge and scampered up the other side. I hiked cross country toward the POW camp. It soon became pitch dark and I couldn't see five feet in front of me! I stumbled in and out of enemy gun emplacements and signal stations but managed to get through without sounding the alarm.

I sipped the water from the creeks and streams I crossed. They all had an acidic taste so I kept on walking. Finally, I got to a point I knew across a street from my prison camp. I walked across the street another couple of hundred yards and found a nice grove of trees. There was a stream there and that water tasted so good. I was going to hide there until our troops came through the area.

I waited for almost a week. The Germans still didn't get overrun by our troops. I didn't have any food. I had diarrhea and I wasn't feeling very good. I said I have to give up. I walked back on the road in broad daylight with my POW overcoat. I walked to the gate to the German guard and said, "Let me in." He said no. An officer came who could speak English. He wanted to know who I was and what I was trying to do getting back in camp. So I told him, "Remember that column that left about a week ago. I was in that column and I got lost and I got sick so here I am." He didn't believe me, but he put me in with a bunch of Air Force officers who were captured. We were rescued. Our troops finally came about a day and half later. We were all glad that the war was over.

Interviewed by Debby Abe and Pei Pei Sung.

Jimmie Kanaya and Beans Sogioka at Camp Crowder, Mo., 1942.
–Courtesy of Jimmie Kanaya.

Shiro KASHINO (1922-1997)

World War II
Army, 442nd Regimental Combat Team, 1943-1945
Staff Sergeant

We were shocked when the radio announced that Japan had attacked Pearl Harbor. I guess everyone was surprised that we had been attacked. It had quite an effect on most Americans of Japanese ancestry because the sentiment was quite bad against the Japanese. I know that we had a lot of racial slurs made at us. I remember having many fights.

[Before all Japanese Americans were evacuated from the West Coast], we…couldn't go down to the waterfront. We were restricted by curfew not to go out after eight o'clock. I had a China button, which Chinese wore [to distinguish themselves from the Japanese, who were classified as "enemy aliens"]. It did not bother the Chinese. It didn't bother me because with that China button, I went anywhere I wanted to go.

[Kashino and his family were sent to Camp Minidoka. He volunteered to work outside of camp.] I was working in this dairy farm when I heard that President Roosevelt would allow Americans of Japanese ancestry to form a segregated Army unit [442nd Regimental Combat Team]. I came back to camp because I wanted to volunteer with our group. I think if we hadn't joined after the President gave us this opportunity, then it would have been very disastrous…

I had brothers, sisters and a niece in this concentration camp. For them to continue to live there as such – it was a very bleak way of life. To go home and

I realize that Japan bombed the United States but we, as Americans of Japanese ancestry, had nothing to do with that.
—Courtesy of Louise Kashino, 1943.

look at a future of living in these concentration camps – it was awful. I felt we had to prove ourselves, and prove to the Americans that we should be given the opportunity to go out and live like we did before. The evacuation was a very unfortunate thing and it tore all these families apart. We lost everything we had. I realize that Japan bombed the United States but we, as Americans of Japanese ancestry, had nothing to do with that. We had to go prove we were Americans so my brothers, sisters and nieces could live a normal life again. This life in camp, it's hard to explain the camp life if you haven't been through it. It was something you wouldn't wish on anybody.

Fighting in Europe

When the 442nd was first exposed to combat, there wasn't too much publicity about it. We had a lot of casualties. In fact, I was wondering how we were going to replace all our wounded and killed in that first drive. We lost 16 from the Seattle area. That's not counting the wounded. We all got together for a silent memorial service. Then we read the Minidoka area paper and we read about the No-No Boys. [The nickname came from their answers to questions about their loyalty to the United States and their willingness to serve in U.S. military.] These were fellows in Minidoka who we knew, had played sports with, and they refused to go into the Army. The publicity they received was tremendous. The thing that hit us the hardest was that we had lost so many from Seattle, not only wounded but actually killed. All this news came out at the same time and most of us felt real bitter about this…because all these guys were killed, but the names of these No-No Boys was a larger headline.

The Lost Battalion was this whole division, four times the size of our regiment. [The battalion had been trapped by the Germans.] They couldn't go save their own battalion so they called us in. We lost more men than we saved. The publicity we received when we did save them was tremendous. Then again, I say we were at the right place, at the right time, and we had a chance to make a name for ourselves. A lot of good outfits in the United States Army were doing good things, but they probably weren't at the right place where they had the chance to make a name for themselves. Our casualties were tremendous. My platoon was the lead platoon in that drive. I lost my platoon in a day or so. I got hit twice.

[After being released from the hospital], I went to join the outfit down there in southern France. I had my platoon again and we had one section to guard. We went to this bar and I knew all of them in the bar. Then a squad of MPs entered the bar and told us to get the hell off the dance hall and bar. My men refused to leave and the MPs pulled their guns out. The next thing you know, all the MPs were busted up. We all had a big fight. I took my platoon and we went back to our area and went to sleep. The next morning, the provost marshal, the head of the jail, with my colonel and about 30 MPs (military police) came down and put my whole platoon in jail. And that's when I was in the stockade, in solitary. [Because a soldier in his platoon wouldn't confess to hitting an officer, Kashino was held responsible for his subordinates' behavior.]

The outfit went back to Italy. Mark Clark was our general. He wanted us back because…a division was stuck at the Gothic Line on the Arno River [the German stronghold]. This was early part of '45 and I was in the stockade. I got orders that I was to be taken out of the stockade…I went back to Italy with the outfit. I was under confinement until they said we were going to make the attack, and then they released me from the jail, the prison stockade. And I took over my platoon on the initial attack on the Gothic Line.

The Army couldn't crack the Gothic Line for six months and the 442nd cracked it in one day. It's just a mountain that the Germans reinforced with cement and stuff and they had artillery. The Americans had bombed it and everything, but they couldn't penetrate that thing. So that night, I remember, we moved up this line. All night, we walked this back trail. It's hard to believe that many men walked up there at night. We had guys who would drop or lose their helmets. Guys would be falling down. Sheer cliffs we walked up! We finally got up there after all that and we made the attack. We kicked them off and we drove them all away. That's what broke the battle line in Italy. We went all the way until the Germans gave up in Italy.

Defending honor

When the war was over, they court-martialed me because of my fight in France. The last drive in Italy, the colonel called…and said if I pled guilty on what he said happened in France, he would give me a lighter sentence. If I pled not guilty, he would give me the general court martial. That's the worst. This captain I was with was a senior officer in charge who knew the charge against me. He said, "Kash, plead not guilty. Hell, you're out, you'll never stand a trial. We'll go back and fight it together." I told the colonel, "Hey, why should I plead guilty when I'm not guilty." Within a week, the captain was killed. So I had nobody to back me up when they went to court martial me. There was nobody to back me up because they were dead. [Kashino later appealed the decision. A few months after his death in 1997, the Army overturned the court martial.]

This was September of '45 when I got home. I came back…to Seattle to see if I could get a job over here and the union wouldn't even hire me. I went down to the local here and they said they were saving jobs for the returning veterans. And I said, "What the hell do you think I am?"

In 1949, we went to West Seattle and they said they wouldn't sell to Japanese. We went to Greenlake and they thought we were Italian with our name Kashino. We walked up and the real estate agents saw we're Japanese; they wouldn't even show us the house.

Interviewed by Debbie Kashino McQuilken and Bev Kashino, courtesy of Seattle Sansei.

–Courtesy of Louise Kashino, 1944.

Richard Lew KAY

Korean War
Army, Quartermaster Corps, 1951-1953
1st Lieutenant

I had two older brothers in World War II. I sort of looked up to them and I wanted to emulate them and somehow be in the Army some day too. I wanted to be like them. I was also proud of what my mother was doing, selling war bonds and helping the war effort.

My second brother enlisted in the Army and was in the Signal Corps. He went over to Australia and New Guinea. And my oldest brother went to college and enrolled in the Reserve Officer Training Corps (ROTC) program and he came out as a lieutenant. He went into the Army Air Corps and lost his life in an Army transport in the Mediterranean, going from the states to North Africa. A German submarine sunk the transport.

After high school, I enrolled at the University of Washington. And then, on the side, I enrolled in the ROTC like my brother did. When I graduated with my degree, I also got a reserve commission in the Army. The Korean War broke out about a year before I graduated so I was kind of expected to go. I was called to active duty after I graduated. I was pretty excited. I was proud to be able to serve my country like my brothers.

I had two older brothers in World War II. I sort of looked up to them and I wanted to emulate them and somehow be in the Army some day too.

Supporting the front lines

I was in the Quartermaster Corps. That's not one of the combat arms of the Army. Combat arms consists of the Infantry, Artillery, and the Armor Corps; they're mostly considered what you call the front lines. Quartermaster is more behind the lines. Their role is to give direct support to the front line. I was a supply officer and we were in to supplies and services for the GIs in the front line. We tried to do the best we could for the personnel. Some of them came back from the lines for rest; we had a lot of these services to make them feel at home. The only time I would see enemy personnel at all would be an occasional sniper. Someone would sneak across the line, infiltrate to the rear and create a little havoc from the rear lines. Sometimes they'd blow up facilities and things like that. Other than that, I had little direct contact. It wasn't a really glorious job. A lot of people don't know that, but the Army figures it takes about maybe seven or eight regular soldiers in the rear to support one infantryman or one man in combat arms, so that's eight-to-one ratio.

Graves registration, that's another job of the Quartermaster Corps. You had to tag the bodies and take off their dog tags. Every soldier wore these so-called dog tags, little metal registration panels that you'd wear around your neck like a necklace. If something happened to the soldier, you could take these dog tags off, document them and do paperwork on them, then send them back to the states. Just part of the job called graves registration. When I first went over there and came in contact with this, of course it was very surprising and depressing. I was sort of taken aback by it. But then I got used to it — didn't make as big an impression anymore. But the first time I was exposed to it, it made an impression.

I worked in maintenance services sometimes. It was enjoyable in a way — kept you busy. Didn't have too much time to think about unpleasant things.

Coming home

During the war, I kept in touch with my family by writing. At the time I was coming back, they were there in Seattle to meet the troop ship coming in. I can remember that. It took about two weeks on troop transport from Korea. It was a pretty good-sized welcome. In those days, the Port of Seattle was used to having troop ships coming back. They had a set routine, a set ceremony for all the troop ships coming back. They had small bands and minor celebrities greeting them. My mom and one of my brothers were there. There were a lot of other people greeting the transport because there were 1,500 soldiers on the troop transport coming back and they all had their families to meet them. It was just quite a joyous experience coming back.

I was in the reserves for about six months after that. Then I got out of the reserves and I went back to school again. Under the GI bill for veterans, if they wanted to go back to school again, they could use the GI bill for three to four years to pay for part of the education. I went back to school and used the GI bill to take pharmacy. I had an interest in pharmacy because of some of my experiences in Korea; we did a lot of work for some of the mobile hospitals, Mobile Army Surgery Hospital (MASH). We did a lot of the work for them, a lot of the baking, cooking and the laundry facilities. We'd launder a lot of their bed sheets and surgeon gowns and what not. Lots of times, I ate meals with some of the personnel who worked in the hospital. Got to talking. Got to know some of the surgeons, dentists and nurses in the hospital there and also met a couple of pharmacists. I got interested in the profession and I gave it a try.

My children never did ask me too much about the war. Actually, my grandson recently talked to me. He's only eight or nine years old. They had a school project on Veterans Day and each person in class was supposed to interview a veteran. They had various questions they were supposed to ask veterans and he came and interviewed me. My grandson was the first one to even ask me about the Korean War. That was quite something.

The public doesn't know much about the Korean War, probably not as much as World War II. It got a bit more publicity. Korean and Vietnam Wars were not publicized as much. Not a lot of people know as much about those two wars. Now more information is coming out. There's a lot more interest in grade school. With this new generation of children, they're more and more interested, more enlightened on the various wars.

I thought the military was a positive experience. I learned a lot about human life in general, the value of human life, and how to interact and deal with people. All the experiences I had, I think, made a better person of me, more tolerant of people. It was quite an education — not only learning how to deal with people, but geographically too. I never traveled out of the United States, other than Canada, 'til then. It was quite an experience.

Interviewed by Pei Pei Sung.

Howard KIM

Vietnam War
Army, 1st Engineer Battalion, 1963-1966; 1975-1978
Specialist E-4

The Army put me in 12-B-10, which was demolition specialists. When I went to Vietnam, I had no training in explosives. I had to learn the hard way. And I did – got hurt a couple of times.

I remember one time when McCracken [demolition partner] and I had to defuse a 50-pound napalm bomb. We found one inside a tank and the two guys inside the tank were dead, but there was what we believed to be a live bomb in there. I had to go down and lift and carry it, and if I dropped it, I would've been gone. We got down on our knees and he was going to do the defusing so I had to hold the cap in… make sure that the thing didn't pop off too soon. He unscrewed the thing and it kind of came loose slowly and he slowly, very slowly released pressure on the spring on the inside. And I was waiting for him to tell me: "Okay! You can let go." And we sweated. We sweated. But finally he said, "Okay Howard, you can let go now." I let go and it just dropped off and the pressure was removed from the inside. There was gunpowder in there, but the thing was defused. McCracken and I walked away and I told McCracken, "I'm shaking and I'm sweating." And McCracken said, "Me, too." I'm still scared thinking about it because I shook for a long time.

Here we are throwing away people like rubbish. I felt like I threw my family in there. These people looked like me. I looked like them.

When we got to one area for a mission, with a bivouac, you have to dig your own…foxhole. It's hard. I took my shirt off; I took my wet gear and my packs off and everything…laid it on the ground against the tree. And then I dug my own foxhole. I was about half way through and I heard something fall from behind. I turned around and P.J. Miller had just knocked a Browning Automatic Rifle off the hands of an Australian trooper. The Australian was going to kill me. He thought that I was a Vietcong. I looked at P.J. and I was so thankful that he was there. And I looked at the Australian and I didn't even want to look at him anymore. How could he be so damn dumb and stupid? If I were a Vietcong, what in the world would I be doing in the middle of an American unit with my shirt off digging a foxhole?

'They looked like me'

About 1:30 one morning, we heard infantry…firing. About the crack of dawn, when all the firing stopped, we had to look for any enemy in the immediate area. We had walked about a couple hundred yards, there was already a bucket loader up front. They had already dug a hole…and they had these dump trucks, one of which I came out there on, with these corpses.

They gave us fatigue pant legs to put on our arms for protection. And then we'd grab these bodies and swing them out far enough so that they won't just fall on the wall of the crater, but they would drop in the middle. And we would toss approximately 100 corpses there, and then stop and then send the dozer down into the crater to shovel dirt over, make another layer and same thing: shovel dirt over it. Make another layer until we had maybe 300, 350 bodies in there. There was a Black guy who was on the other side of the crater. He too was on the detail. Everybody else was Caucasian. And I felt overwhelmed. Here we are, we're throwing away people like rubbish…I felt like I threw my family in there. These people looked like me. I looked like them.

Abuse of power

I remember George. He had 16 years in the Army. He was kind of powerfully built, he was strong and he was intimidating. He grabbed me by the hand one night, took me across the field to one of his friends in another unit and had me drink cognac with him. And I was scared of him. I mean, I was intimidated. He grabbed me by my wrists and took me across the field, took me to my own pup tent. Then he raped me in the tent. I couldn't stop him.

I think that one of the reasons why I wanted to come home from Vietnam – other than my fear of the war itself – I wanted to get away from George. I didn't want to be in the same squad or platoon with George because there was the threat there that I felt. He threatened me one time if I told anybody what he did, that he would kill me. I was scared of that.

I'll probably never see George again. Then, I still have these flashbacks. I have flashbacks of the burial. I have flashbacks of being shot at. I have flashbacks of shooting people. I have flashbacks of just being there.

As the years went by, I wanted to resurrect George and kill him. And bring him back and kill him and bring him back and kill him and bring him back and kill him. And then I realized the problem was not George; it was me. The only way I could drop it, the only way that I could at least get myself half the healing was to say, "Howard, you gotta to forget George, you gotta to forgive him. You gotta to let go of it."

Coming home

I felt more suicidal after the war. I had mixed feelings when leaving Vietnam because I kept thinking of my friends who died over there. I thought about my friends who survived, but I was probably never going to see again. I wept in the plane because I could see the lights going farther and farther down.

I went and I sought counseling when I first got out in the '60s. They didn't know what it was that I had. Why was I reliving these things over and over again? It's emotional scars that stay there. Some people say scars don't hurt, but there are some scars that hurt. The emotional kind does.

When I had gone to the VA (Veterans Affairs), I had gone in and asked where's the psychiatrist at. I told him I had some problems…some emotional problems. I just couldn't get over the war. He asked me, "Do you have flashbacks?" And I told him: "No, I don't know what a flashback is." Then he said, "There's nothing wrong with you."

I was living in a…condemned building. When I came home from the VA office, I got so frustrated. I saw somebody burning a pile of rubbish. Maybe I could throw away some things I don't even need. I got these certificates, these are nothing but tokens, these are certificates of appreciation. They give this stupid medal. It's nothing but a medal. This is the way the government helps me out when I need help? I can't even hold on a job. I can't support myself. I stormed into the VA office one day and said, "Look, why did you guys bring me home, and not provide me a way to take care of my own self? If I stayed in the military, if you kept me over there, so things are dangerous, at least I would have gotten paid and I could sustain myself. Now I'm over here and I'm a homeless vet. I have no way to pay my rent, I don't even have a job, except driving a cab. I have no pension. I have nothing."

Interviewed by Debby Abe and Bianca Chinn.

Spady KOYAMA

World War II, Korean War and Vietnam War
Army, Military Intelligence Service, 1942-1945; 1947-1970
Colonel

[After the bombing of Pearl Harbor], my mother takes me aside and…says, "I needn't tell you that this is your country, no matter who says what. Now your country is at war. You should be mentally prepared to go fight for your country."

On Jan 5, 1942, I walked to the selective service office where an official told me, "You better go home and think things over first. We're at war with Japan, you know." I said, "I know. That's why I'm here." And he kept telling me to go home…I wasn't exactly angry; I was disturbed more than angry. I finally pushed a piece of paper across the top of the desk and said, "Print your name on this piece of paper and give me the names of the rest of you fellows in this…office. If they tell me in Fort Lewis that I don't qualify, then I will come home, but you fellows…don't even want to send me over there. Human interest story. I'm going give it to one of my buddies who works for a newspaper." He went back and told the others about it. He came back and said, "Well, don't blame us if something happens to you." I said, "Oh, no. Just send me out of here." At Camp Murray, I raised my right hand to be sworn in as a buck private earning $21 a month on Jan. 8, 1942 – a month and a day after Pearl Harbor.

I raised my right hand to be sworn in as a buck private earning $21 a month on January 8th, 1942, a month and a day after Pearl Harbor.

After basic training at Camp Roberts, Calif., I got on the military truck and was driven down to the railroad station. I noticed about seven other Orientals. I thought they can't be all going to the same school I'm going to. Some of them don't look too bright. A long train came in, shutters pulled down and an MP (military policeman) jumped off and told us to get on. Lo and behold, everybody on board was a Nisei soldier in uniform and some of them had stripes. The train started pulling out and wouldn't stop until…Oklahoma. By that time, some of the soldiers were getting nervous and, in fact, one fellow said, "You don't suppose this train is going to stop in the middle of nowhere and we'll be ordered to get off and have a bunch of machine guns pointing at us?" About that time, some names were called off and, to the relief of the rest of us, some of the fellows got off. When the train finally hit Little Rock, Ark., my name was called and I wound up at Camp Joseph T. Robinson to finish my basic training.

Mistaken for dead

I finished training in the Military Intelligence Service School and Camp Savage, Minn., and was shipped out. I participated in the invasion of the Philippines. Our landing ship tank was bombed Oct. 25, 1944. From the ricochet, hot bits embedded in my face and the main piece knocked my helmet off. I was wearing sunglasses, which protected my eyeballs apparently, but the rim caught me between my eyes. Blood was running into my right eye and so I couldn't see…nor could I hear out of my broken eardrum. There were 26 of us wounded seriously enough so that we were left side by side…on a beach at Leyte Island, our objective. At first, I thought, "Why are we out here in the open beach? We could get strafed any moment." Then I thought we were all waiting to get treated medically. Then I thought I lost my left ear and my right eye because I couldn't hear and I couldn't see. I took my right arm and checked my face and I was pleased to notice I had my left ear and my right eyeball. That's where my good Lord interceded and said, "Don't put your arm down by your side where it was. Leave it on your chest." So I left it on my chest and apparently out of 26 bodies, everybody's arm was down except there's one short Oriental with his arm on his chest. To make a long story short, I never got buried with the rest of them. I was taken out of there. I eventually was sent to California for surgery. The surgery failed in that the shrapnel piece is still in my right chest.

Unexpected friendship

In 1944, I was interrogating prisoners who would come in to the POW camp in Dutch New Guinea Prefecture. Whenever they came in, we went through a sort of recruiting procedure; we would line them up and have them take their uniform off. At the same time, I would go down the line with a pack of cigarettes in one hand and a lighter in the other, offer each man a cigarette and explain that we will issue a new uniform as soon as they go wash up. I came across this one big fellow. I offered him a cigarette and he turned that away. I thought, well this guy doesn't smoke. I kept on going down the line and as I returned passed him, he suddenly stuck out his hand. So I gave him a cigarette and lit it for him and I told one of my associates, "Save that big guy for me. I want to talk to him."

A couple of days later, I finally got to this fellow, Yoshio Takayama from Kagoshima. I asked him, "How come you refused my cigarette when I first came down?" He said, "At first, I thought if this is a place of execution I would not even accept a cigarette from that man. And then as you went down the line, I heard everyday Japanese being spoken in a normal tone of voice somewhere." And so he thought, this couldn't be a place of execution…and took the cigarette when I came back again.

Later, I nominated Takayama to be in charge of leading a work crew of prisoners. I told Takayama, "We have warehouse where Japanese food is. You appoint a man to be in charge of the cooking area." And he did. We would sometimes go on our own and eat with them. That relationship continued until…sometime in September 1944. We suddenly got orders to start packing.

As I was helping to break down the tent outside the compound, Takayama came to the gate and motioned for me. He said, "I have one final request to make. I know you're leaving. I would like to know your name and address so that possibly after the war, I could properly thank you for all your kindness." I was surprised. I thought I was just doing my job. I said, "You know I can't give you my name and address." He looked so disappointed so I said, "Look, if I survive and get to Japan, I know who you are and you come from Kagoshima and I can look for you." So with that, we parted and I took off and got on board this LST, landing ship tank 552. To many of us Army personnel, LST stood for Large Slow Target.

In 1949, I'm in Japan and one day I'm going passed the Army Demobilization Bureau and the thought enters my mind: I promised Takayama in 1944…that I would look him up if I ever got to Japan. I drove my jeep into the bureau…and spoke to the headman, who was just flabbergasted about this strange relationship between a Japanese prisoner and an American. And he said, "This is the Army Demobilization Bureau. The man you're interested in is a Navy man. However, I would be honored if you would give us the task of finding that man for you." In three days, he had him. I told the official to find out the time and day of Takayama's arrival in Tokyo so I could provide the round-trip train fare. The day finally arrived and I went down to Tokyo railroad station and there was a big crowd. I came across Takayama seated on the floor. Everybody was walking around, gawking at him. He had inquired around to public officials; nobody knew what to wear to Tokyo. So he thought, "I can't go wrong if I wear part of my uniform." Everybody was milling around him, wondering where this guy came from, wearing part of a defeated Navy uniform? I went inside and approached him. He looked up, recognized me instantly. Big tears welled in his eyes and I quickly took him out of there, took him to the nearest clothing store and made him look more presentable.

Years later, Takayama came to visit me in Spokane. Apparently, I'm the only one who ever had…a former prisoner interrogated overseas during wartime, saw fit to save his money for so many years — from 1944 to 1989 — and then to come over at his own expense to visit me.

Interviewed by Tom Ikeda, courtesy of Densho Project.

Bert C. LETRONDO, SR.

World War II, Korean War and Vietnam War
Navy, USS Piedmont #1817; USS Eversole #DDR 789, 1946-1967
Yeoman 1st Class

In 1941, I was a 17 year-old student at the Visayan Institute in Cebu City, Philippines. But then the war came on Dec. 7 when Japanese forces devastated Pearl Harbor in Hawaii. When the news spread…that the Japanese was also going to invade the Philippines…they closed all schools and they sent all the students home. In April 1942, the first Japanese contingent was sent to our hometown of Palompon in…Leyte. During the first few days of the Japanese occupation, the soldiers would try to convince the people…that they were not conquerors but liberators. [At that time, the Philippines was a territory of the United States.] When the Japanese soldiers realized that there were townfolks…opposed to their occupation, they started treating them like animals, beating them with guns, raping women and forcing both young and old men to act as their guides during patrols.

We, in our hometown, organized a guerrilla force. It was so secret that nobody, except those who joined… knew that there was an organization trying to oppose…the Japanese. To join, you went through a very strict investigation and you had to sign a piece of paper with your blood: "We now belong to the guerrilla forces." To start with, we didn't have arms. Our

We, in our hometown, organized a guerrilla force. To join you had to sign a piece of paper with your blood: 'We now belong to the guerrilla forces.'

weapons were just strictly homemade from water pipes and wire fence. We used slingshots…with poisoned arrows. It was required that before we were issued a weapon – I really hate to mention this – we had to bring a Japanese head to the commander. That's how we get our weapons.

I was 18 then. So then our activities, as assigned to us by the regional commander, were to either ambush or give information about the Japanese movement. My brother, Enrique, and I were in the same group when we ambushed several patrols. Me being the youngest of all the seven children, my mom didn't want me to join. She asked our commander if I could be reassigned with my oldest brother, Vicente, who was in the intelligence group.

In October 1945, when the American liberation forces landed in Leyte, some of us were detached and were assigned to a rehabilitation group, which was building makeshift cottages for hundreds of displaced war victims.

After the war, schools were reopened and…high school graduates were trained to teach grades one through seven. I taught the first and third grades for a while until I learned that the U.S. Navy was recruiting Filipinos. I told the superintendent of school that I would like to resign because I would like to join the Navy. This was in 1945. I was able to convince my friend, Andres Cainap, to come with me. I told him, "Let's go for an adventure…This is one of my dreams. I want to see the U.S.A."

We found out when we went to Tatloban that…the recruiting headquarters moved to Manila. Meanwhile, we found a job working for the 77th American Division with Col. Andrew Shanks as our boss. He was kind enough to offer Andres and me free air transportation to Nichols Air Base in Manila where the recruitment office was. Col. Shanks said, "If you still need help, you know where we are…Don't hesitate." I said, "Colonel, the best thing you can do, if you don't mind, is…give me a letter of recommendation that I worked for you." Because of Col. Shanks' written recommendation, I finally realized my dream of joining the U.S. Navy. I didn't know what I was going to be. For a month, we were in Manila and then they put us…aboard *USS Los Angeles* going to Yokusoka, Japan. Still, I didn't know what I was going to be doing because we were what they called "transients" until we got our permanent station. While in Japan, we were just passengers. I thought, "This is the kind of life I want. You get up, go eat your meal, go to bed." But during the day, of course, they assigned us to do chores, chip paint or whatever. And I still didn't know what I was going to be doing. And then we got to Japan and we got our orders. That's when I knew what I was going to be doing in the Navy: steward. I was teaching before I came in the Navy…then all of a sudden, I was in the steward's branch, working for officers, serving food.

All the Filipinos who came into the Navy during those years, from '46 to '65, went straight to the stewards branch…they serve food, they cook, they clean officers' quarters…shine shoes. I did that for two years…During those years…it was hard to change rate. To get out of the stewards branch was very hard. When I was stationed to the destroyer *USS Eversole*, they assigned me to work for the captain. So one time, he saw me in his quarters using his typewriter…typing a short letter to my folks back home. I was scared because I thought maybe he was going to can me! I was shaking. I said, "Captain, I'm sorry. I didn't mean to use your typewriter." He said, "Son, don't worry. Do what you're doing now, and if there's anything I can do, let me know."

Later, he asked me, "Are you interested to change rate?" Boy! The whole world just lit up, you know. I said, "Like what rate, Captain?" He said, "Well, I saw you typing. Would you be interested to be in the clerical rate?…When you finish your job…I will tell the chief that you will be working there part-time in the personnel office." In my mind, I said, "Thank you, Lord."

I worked in the personnel office, in the yeoman section of it…so in two months, approval from the bureau came in that changed my rate from steward to seaman. As soon as you changed your rate to seaman, you could change your rate [to other positions]. So in my case, I was interested in becoming the yeoman; it would give me a chance to use my head!

I know in our squadron, and from other ships I visited, I can only recall five Filipino seamen out of a whole bunch, like 200, 300 Filipinos. So advancement had to depend on the benevolence of the captain. If you didn't have a connection, you didn't have a chance.

Interviewed by Eydie Detera.

—*Courtesy of Bert C.Letrondo, Sr., 1946.*

Dec. 1946

Raymond LEW

World War II
Army, Headquarters Company, 7th Infantry Division, 1943-1946
Sergeant

My brother's classmate was in the military in China and he talked to us. And, of course, we were young men and impressionable, and he told us about his duties as a soldier and military man in China with the Chinese Army and they were fighting the Japanese in those days. And so there was, of course, Errol Flynn and the war movies. And I was a great reader of adventure and I read a great many books on World War I pilots and the fighters.

Enlistment was…an adventure. My history teacher was a graduate of Annapolis and one of our alumni was Col. Magnuson, and a few came back and spoke at our school assemblies. The spirit of war was raging to a high fervor, to a high pitch and being patriotic and all this, why, this was the thing to be a part of. Knowing my eyes were bad, I did to go the Navy recruiting office to have them check my eyes, and, no, they were just too bad and they wouldn't take me. I just waited until I turned 18 and registered for the draft and I was selected and I hadn't finished high school. So I went to war…before getting my high school degree.

I was 18 years old, healthy and eager and looking for adventure, as any 18 year old would. I was training with the heavy weapons, that means the machine gun, .30 caliber machine gun and the 80 millimeter mortars. We carried that all around the desert. They were heavy, but the other fellows were young too.

I just waited until I turned 18 and registered for the draft. I was selected and I hadn't finished high school. So I went to war…before getting my high school degree.

At basic training, we had no idea what was going to happen. We knew we were being trained and going to be sent elsewhere. Our lives depended upon the training we received and how well we did in training. We were 18 and those young people make the best soldiers.

I didn't have any thoughts about what would happen after. Maybe my parents did. Nothing's going to happen to me. I'm not going to die. I'll come back. I was quite certain of that. And the young people today still believe that. When you're that age, "I won't ever get caught," you know. The young people today are just as cocky as before.

En route overseas, we stopped at a couple of places along the way. And when I was in Hawaii, a Seattlite, Warren Chan and I hooked up. On the way to the Philippines, we landed on one of the South Pacific islands, and he looked me up again. He was able to make it through once more in the Philippines. He was with the signal company, and he knew where I was. After the battle, he looked me up again. It was nice to see someone from the hometown. After the Philippine battle, we went to Okinawa, and his unit came along, and after the battle there, he looked me up. It was great that we survived the war.

Once we landed in the Philippines, we lived in tents when we could. There was no other facility; we lived, we slept on the ground. It was the monsoon season. Rain, never saw rain like that – just deep, ankle deep in mud. I recall saying, "God, I wonder if the people back home appreciate why I'm out here in this muck and mud." Everything was wet. Crazy, it was. You didn't cheer yourself up. I mean, this was life, this was the way it was. You just lived with it.

One night, "Bed Check Charlie" [a nickname for enemy planes flying at night] came over and dropped a bomb and hit our supply of ammunition and it blew right up. This is in the evening, of course, and it was just a complete mess. There was not so much panic, but chaos. I had already taken off my shirt, my pants, and crawled into my sleeping bag. The next thing I knew, the tent collapsed and everybody was yelling. There was a fire burning. Something was burning and the first things I reached for were my pants and my shoes.

Then I called for my friends; they weren't around. There was always talk about a counterattack by the enemy and so be ready, have your gun ready and all this. I couldn't find anyone. Then, all of a sudden, I felt a very burning sensation. I didn't know what it was, just on my back, a burning sensation. I shrugged it off and kept on moving. I found out later that I was hit by shrapnel.

All I had were my pants, my shoes, no weapon, 'cause I couldn't find it, and I was crawling around in the dark, because, word is:…keep down, don't stand up because who knows what can happen. I crawled around the box and there was a soldier there, a White soldier, and he had his pistol and all I could see was the muzzle of that .45 caliber automatic weapon. 'Cause he was around the box and I didn't know he was there, and he didn't know I was coming around the box. And with my GI haircut and my suntan, and I didn't have my glasses on…I couldn't see worth anything. "Wait, I'm not a Jap," I said. For some reason, he didn't do anything either. He said, "Okay, crawl over." He wants to see me. And what can you see? You see an Asian body with a pair of dirty pants and shoes, I could be the enemy. I had my dog tags…but he stilled looked at me real hard. And all I could see was this automatic weapon he had. But I showed him my tags…and he said "okay." He moved on.

I crawled around and I reached into a duffel bag. I opened it because I wanted a shirt, I wanted a fatigue jacket. I didn't know whose bag I had opened. I just took it out and I put it on. Then I saw a White soldier who I knew. We recognized each other and I said, "Wait for me. I want to join you." So I walked with him for the rest of that morning. Every time I walked by, people were looking at me. I said, "Why are they looking at me?" He said, "Well the jacket you have on is a captain's jacket." I was a private first class.

I was hoping to get into the medical field when I came out of the service. So I said, "Well, gosh, why don't I go to join the medical unit." I put in a request. And they were just next door. I had friends in both areas, I had friends in the kitchen, had friends in the medics. The medics had the alcohol and the kitchen had the food, and I had friends in both areas, so you want to trade? So you see, my tour really was not horrible.

In the medical unit, I was supposed to just be on call to offer assistance to give shots. The troops would come by, you give them shots. And so this one guy said, "Oh Ray, it's your turn, give 'em shots." They all lined for the shots. So I took this hypodermic and the needle and shot, shot, shot. And then I said, "Oh my God, I'm supposed to change needles." I learned quickly and they taught me how to fix cough syrup for those who needed it. And I was able to make my own Vitalis hairdressing.

I can't say that my experience matured me a great deal other than the normal maturation process. I can't say that I was wiser and more thoughtful or anything like that. I was still young and cocky. I didn't see what other soldiers saw. I saw the dead enemy but I didn't see the killing. I didn't see any of that. The experiences others have – I don't deny them their experiences. I'm glad I wasn't there. "I'm sorry it was you, but better you than me" – this type of thing. During World War II, some of my friends were stationed in Hawaii throughout their service time. They came home like a regular eight-hour job, but they were in the service. They did their part too.

Each war has been different…but it's not different for those who were in the front line. They died. They were hurt. Politically, for the government and for the people at home, each war is a different war. Well, yes, but people still died.

Interviewed by Carina A. del Rosario.

Raymond Lew (l) and Warren Chan, both from Seattle, run into each other by chance in Hawaii before their tour of duty overseas, 1944.
—Courtesy of Raymond Lew.

James LOCKE

World War II
Army, 5th Armor Division, 1941-1945
Staff Sergeant

I was drafted before Pearl Harbor – 1940, I believe. I went to Fort Lewis. There were about three of us, three Chinese boys, together went to Fort Lewis. From there we went to Texas, all three of us. When you're drafted, you have to tell what you do, so I said, "I'm a cook." They put me in the kitchen. Then the other Chinese boy, he didn't know too much English. I told the captain: "Hey, my buddy here doesn't know much English, how about putting him with me, so he doesn't have to go out in the field." He put him with me, so he didn't have to go to the front line like all the infantry people. Stay in the kitchen with me.

From Texas after basic training, the 5th Armor Division was just forming in Kentucky, in Fort Knox. They sent us up to Fort Knox to join the 5th Armor Division. We were sent to the service company to carry ammunition, gasoline and what not, and food stuff to the front line. When we get to Fort Knox, there's another Chinese boy in there. So three of us had a good time then, three Chinese boys in the same company.

When we were in Europe, I got promoted as mess sergeant and in charge of officers' mess. And oh, we eat good – steak all the time. We ate New York steak because we took over the hotel there, the officer's mess was in the hotel. The hotel had broilers – fancy hotel – and we had broiled steak, pork chops and what not. We got so much pork, pork loin, that we had to take it up to an English butcher shop, had it ground up to

make sausage for breakfast. And then, as mess sergeant, I had to make three kinds of ice cream every night...and take it up to a English ice cream parlor and...freeze it for the next day. Every day.

In those days, there's no combat yet. It's still before D-Day. And at night time, usually a German V-bomb would come all over the place. Boy, when they came, when you heard the noise, it was okay. But once you didn't hear the noise, you better go down to the basement because that's when they were going to drop them. They really hit us pretty good, but didn't hit the hotel.

During the German offensive there, we almost got blown out of the hilltop. All our supplies were on top of the mountain there, a little hill. There was some spotter plane to see where the enemies were. The Germans captured one of our spotter planes. So we thought it was our own plane, but it was a German plane. They directed all the artillery right on top of us so we had to get the heck out of there in a hurry. Some of the ammunition trucks got blown up and some of the gasoline trucks were blown up.

I got out in 1945. I could've gone to college for four years for nothing – GI bill. But then when I came out of the Army, since I don't too good at school, my dad said, "Ah, don't go to school. When you get through school, you probably come out as a cook anyway!"

After a few years, I went to Hong Kong. A friend said, "Hey Jimmy. You want I introduce you to a beautiful girl?" I said, "Okay." He knew my future wife's family well so he introduced me at their house. I went to the American consulate in Hong Kong, witness for the marriage. In those days, if you were a GI, you got married, you could bring your bride right over, same time. You didn't even have to wait.

Interviewed by Ron Chew and John D. Pai.

In those days, if you were a GI and you got married, you could bring your bride right over. You didn't even have to wait.

Douglas LUNA

Vietnam War
Air Force, 35th Infantry Combat Support Group, 1963-1966
Airman 1st Class, E-4

After high school, I wasn't ready for college and nothing here in civilian life appealed to me at that time...So it was a little bit of wander lust [that led to enlisting in the Air Force].

When I first decided to go into the service, I was going to join the Navy. My dad and my grandfather were both in the Navy, and I had one uncle in the Navy. I went down to talk to the Navy recruiter and the guy looked at me and said, "Hey, you're part Filipino. How well do you like to cook?" I said forget that mess. I went to talk to the Marines and they kept showing me all these pictures about camping outdoors all the time. That didn't enthuse me a whole lot...I went over to talk to the Army and because I'm bilingual, they were interested in me, but I wasn't that interested in them. So I joined the Air Force.

Up in the air

The first time I saw anti-aircraft fire come up, I was a volunteer "flare kicker." I thought, "Hey, that's sort of pretty." Just like in the movies. The thing is, you saw very few tracers coming up at you because they used very few. And I suddenly realized: That sucker's shooting at me. We were only flying at about 800 feet.

I couldn't participate in the pro-war or anti-war movements. I lost too many friends in Vietnam who thought they were doing the right thing.

I remember my third mission was probably the most traumatic. Our dinner was creamed chicken on toast. We got above the mountains and this camp was being hit pretty bad. So we were flying cover, and there were some very severe wind drafts, and we were just really being buffeted. I got sick and everyone else got sick on the aircraft. We threw out the barf bags after we threw out our flares. Everyone swore that the next time when we came back, the anti-aircraft fire increased. We always joked that maybe somebody down there on the ground got hit in the head with a barf bag and he just got mad.

I think it was on this same mission, when one camp was hit. There were 81 bodies in and around the camp...my lighting up the sky, to a certain extent, led to the death of 81 people. That was the first time I realized I helped kill 81 people. When you'd see intelligence photos of targets, you never looked at the targets as human beings in a building. It was "The Target." Just like if you listen to the aircraft pilots talk, they talk about knocking out the tank. They don't talk about killing the people inside. And maybe it's a defensive mechanism that you have in order to do the job.

I had a friend of mine, Maj. Geoffords. In December of '65 – it was about six hours before the truce went into effect – our commanders sent a lone gun ship, a spook, into a valley where they knew that there was a radar controlled gun. Geoffords got whacked to the sky. It's stupid to send an aircraft out, not knowing exactly where that gun is, but knowing you're going to try to knock it out. He never had a chance. They never did find his aircraft or any of the guys. To see something like that, that's what made me sort of bitter about the war. The main reason I got out was that I saw too many people getting wasted.

On guard

Your basic reaction was not to trust any civilian. During that '66 Tet celebration, I was sitting in a bar having a drink and the kids had been throwing off firecrackers outside. I heard the screen door open very slowly, and I could smell a fuse, and I cleared leather [drew gun out of the holster] – and I wasn't the only one. One of the tricks used to be to open the door, throw in a grenade and leave…but it was some little kid with a firecracker in his hand. He stood there and then he saw the guns. Then he stopped, froze and the firecracker went off in his hands. I recognize how close I came to killing the little kid, but at the same time, I had made a conscious decision when I went for my weapon that it was me or whoever was coming through that door.

I had a different perspective about Vietnam. Because my stepfather was in the Army, I was an Army brat and we were aware of a lot of people whose fathers were sent to Vietnam in 1961 and '62 out of Germany. And then being involved in the air intelligence and special projects, I was aware of that aspect. So you got a certain amount of bias that maybe we should be there.

To a certain extent, I saw in '65 and '66 a lot of racism because the U.S. military had no concept of dealing with Asians. I mean the theory that the North Vietnamese would not win the war just because we had more weapons and technology than they did. The U.S. military did not recognize the motivation. It was fundamentally stupid to consider that because a person does not have the same materials and training you have that they're inferior. Everyone thought I was going to reenlist except me because after I got there, I recognized how we were going to lose the war. It was a very scary feeling and very powerless to be able to tell your country, "Hey, the way we're going about it, we're going to lose" just because we did not have the hearts and minds of the people. As the war dragged out, my suspicions were confirmed.

At the same time, I couldn't participate in the pro-war or anti-war movements. I lost too many friends in Vietnam in '65 and '66 who thought they

–Courtesy of Douglas Luna, 1965.

were doing the right thing. We were in Da Nang when we saw the first article come out on an anti-war demonstration, and it kind of shook a lot of us because you're going over, you're proud, your country's going to support you. That was the feeling we had. And to see the anti-war demonstration, that concerned us. Maj. Geoffords' comment to me was… "Right or wrong, we've taken an oath to defend the Constitution. They have the right to do whatever they're doing." Two weeks later, he was shot down. He felt he was right doing what he was doing there. He felt he had to follow his obligations. I never forgot that.

[Heading back to the U.S.], I flew out that night on a Flying Tigers' aircraft. It was kind of strange because there was a firefight going on… It was five miles away. I still had my weapon, carried that with me. I cleared my weapon with airport security like a half-hour before I boarded the airplane, and had to check in my bag. It was a strange feeling because when we took off, you could see the gun flashes, and you had to think that maybe they're aiming at you. We landed in Japan for refueling, and then on to Travis Air Force Base, north of San Francisco. We came in. It was raining. It was cold. No bands were playing, no nothing. There were a few people there who had relatives waiting for them. The rest of us — it was like shock. You got off the airplane, you picked up your bags, and here I was, still walking around with a bandoleer of ammunition in my bag and my pistol.

Two days later, the family was waiting at the SeaTac airport, and everyone was glad to see me. It was good, but about two days later, after I had been back, I wasn't used to being bored. Really strange feeling, after working that long for six, six and a half days a week, I had nothing to do. Nobody to order you around.

Interviewed by Ken Mochizuki.

Rosendo LUNA, SR.

World War II
Army, U.S. Philippine Scouts, 14th Combat Engineer, 1937-1958
Sergeant 1st Class

I followed in the footsteps of my father, a professional soldier; he's an old scout who enlisted in 1910, retired 1935. He was stationed in the Philippines. Of 11 siblings, I think there are only three of us living. One died in a bombing by the Japanese during World War II.

I went to Philippine Business College in Manila...then enlisted in the military Army because during that time [1937], the U.S. Army was inducting soldiers in the Philippines. So instead of going into the Philippine Army, I went into the U.S. Army. During that time, you could not find any work.

In 1941, we heard there was a plan of Japanese attack or bombardment, but we didn't expect this would come true. We just kept on training. In November or October, we were issued weapons. That's the time we realized this would be different from what we expected. The training was really getting worse, day and night. We hiked 20 miles walking back and forth, instead of 10 miles like before. On Dec. 3, we heard on the radio that...Japan was planning to attack some country but we didn't know which one. So we just kept on training and training until Dec. 7 when we heard that Pearl Harbor was bombed. Then that was the time when we heard there would be war. On Dec. 8, 1941, three o'clock in the morning,

I followed in the footsteps of my father. He's an old scout who enlisted in 1910, retired 1935.

we heard a bomber... maybe two or three bombers above us. The following morning, we found out the bombers had hit about five miles away from our unit. One of our companies was hit. Three people were killed.

Falling into enemy hands

On one mission, I was driving a truck loaded with ammunition that I had to haul to my unit so that they could use it on the defense line. And the Japanese shelling was occurring in front of me. I told myself, "Well, I'm alone and my unit is on the other side. I might be killed here. I might as well go and leave this truck here." I didn't know how far it was to the other side of the trail so I went with another unit. Most of us were like stragglers now – walking and running around. But I got my rifle gun and that was the only thing I had. Finally, I reached the upper part of my company where there was a regiment. We were not actually captured yet but our commanding officer said, "Okay, you guys either go your own way or you can surrender. Because you are Filipino, maybe the Japanese will not bother you. For us, we are American. We cannot escape."

So finally, some of my friends decided to escape. We went to the kitchen, gathered some rice, gathered some canned foods, gathered everything so that we could bring it to a place we could reach. Finally we went...up to the mountain.

We marched in...a straight line. We passed some rivers and then we started going up some steep mountains. And then finally we reached the low land where there were some farmers living in the houses. We asked them how was the situation on the other side. They said that the Filipinos were given freedom. The

Japanese were sending them away, letting them go. We were a little bit discouraged; we didn't even know if what they were saying was true. So we went to the main road…slowly walking and walking and walking. Then we saw plenty of prisoners walking on the road – Americans, Filipinos, and civilians, followed by tanks, trucks and equipment. "Well, maybe they're going home," we thought. So I said, "Well, maybe we could join them." All of us went to the road and marched. We didn't even know what might happen to us. We thought we were already free. We kept on walking, walking on the road. And finally we stopped. We found out that we were at the first prisoner-of-war (POW) camp.

Bataan Death March

[The Japanese grouped the prisoners to march from one camp to another.] We walked 65 miles in the heat of the sun from Maribeles to San Fernando. I didn't know that we were part of the Bataan Death March. You urinated blood because it was so hot.

While on the road, most everyone complained that they wanted water. They would want to go in the well or ditches, or the wallow place where the carabou drank. But if you moved from the column, the Japanese would bayonet, shoot or club you. You were helpless. And you could die on the march, which many people did.

Later, we were grouped again to be loaded in the boxcar. The boxcar could only hold 100 to 150 people. It was crammed – we were just like sardines there without any ventilation inside the boxcar. You couldn't sit down. You had to stand up. The boxcar filled with stink from urine or some kind of defecated waste. You knew that many people were already sick so it was hard to breathe. If you didn't have the stomach to resist, then you might be one of the dead people there.

Hardships of POW camp

In the POW camp, you didn't really know who was still able bodied because tomorrow they might die. I experienced that. I had two or three friends that I thought could resist the sickness that they had: malaria, beriberi, dysentery and diarrhea. But they died. Most of the POWs were taking all these leaves and cooking, drinking it. This was the only food they could rely on. There was nothing you could eat. I myself ate a dead frog we caught in a ditch. Otherwise, all you had to survive on in the POW camp

was a saucer full of rice, salt and water…not even the Red Cross fed us. There was no Red Cross in the POW camp, no medical treatment, nothing. That's why we got plenty of sickness and disease. Now medicine, if you got money, you lived. If you didn't have money, you died.

I saw my father in the camp after the Bataan Death March. They had a different place where all the retired personnel who had been in the service were concentrated in one area. There were so many old people in the camp ranging from 50 to 80 years of age. They were given some type of work to do, like security. My father was so young, 57, to die in the concentration camp. Just imagine, he was only 57. I still remember that when I saw my father in the concentration camp, he was also helping the sick people. Then after two or three weeks, I never heard from him or saw him anymore. I was surprised when a friend of mine told me that my father was carried to the graveyard. He died of diarrhea, dysentery, malaria, beriberi, every kind of sickness you could get there.

And that was the hardship of the concentration camp. You have a faucet but you don't have any water. The water we had for taking baths was from the drainage which came from the kitchen because that's the only water you could have. Then the water you could use in the kitchen you had to get by walking for two miles away from the concentration camp. You had to carry a 55-gallon drum. Four of us, with a pole tied to the drum, would carry it, guarded by two Japanese soldiers. So we had to walk two miles and then fill the 55-gallon drum and then back again to the POW camp. Just imagine that. Every day.

Interviewed by Ferdinand de Leon and Jose Velasquez.

Dan K. MAR

World War II
Navy, Group Pacific 13, 1943-1946
Electrician 3rd Class

We didn't hear about the bombing of Pearl Harbor until the next day. I was too dang young to really give it a lot of thought. I wasn't that young, but by the same token, these worldly things never occurred to me. And I guess the only thing that really brought it home were the radio messages, like F.D.R. (President Franklin D. Roosevelt)...saying, "Yeah, we're going to go to war and get ready." Of course, I was only 15 at that time so I didn't give a lot of thought to the events or what was going to happen...

I was still going to high school when I was 17-and-a-half, and I was still a sophomore. The ruling was that if you were not at least a senior by the time you were 18, you were eligible for the draft. And so I kind of waited [for the draft notice]...I knew I was going to go in.

It was probably 30 days after I turned 18 when the notice came: "Greetings from the President of the United States. You are to report at so and so at such date for induction into the armed services." So away I went.

When you're young and have no real deep thoughts about war, say that you're going to die or you're going to get killed or whatever the case might be, you kind of took it for face value and said, "Okay, let's go." Everybody else was going. I knew once I got in there, there'd be a certain amount of either firing

My tour of the Navy was just kind of like a 'Gilligan's Island' you might say. It was a lot of fun in a lot of respects and a lot of interesting things happened.

at somebody or somebody firing at you. That's why I...said, "Hey, I'll go in the Navy. Maybe I won't have to face anybody with a gun."

At that time, the Navy was pretty segregated, and they weren't taking very many people of color to serve in the Navy, but I guess by the end of '43, they were really desperate for men. I was the only Chinese in our company of about 60 people in boot camp. I was accepted right off the bat and I had no problems because of race.

I had a terrible time in boot camp. Couldn't swim. They couldn't teach me. I learned how to float — that was the only requirement...If you could float on your back or front to the middle of the pool, climb on the raft, shove off of the side, and get to the other side, you passed the swimming test — whether you swam or not. The last day at boot camp, I finally passed it.

The first Chinese American group in the Navy

My tour of the Navy was just kind of like "Gilligan's Island," you might say. It was a lot of fun in a lot of respects and a lot of interesting things happened. Sure, it was serious, but...later on, when we got transferred to China, we had a lot of fun.

I was transferred to Pearl Harbor, and I didn't know what the duty was or anything, but I walked into this hut and then a guy says, "Take any bunk you want." There were only four people in there. I said, "What's all this about?" He said, "Don't bother us. We're playing mah jong now." As it turned out, it was an all Chinese group. The first time that the Navy had ever formed an ethnic group, other than the Black waiters and stewards and cooks. The irony of the whole thing is the people who they recruited, like myself, spoke the wrong dialect. They gave us…a uniform, gave us a gun, and tried half-heartedly to teach us how to speak Mandarin, which was a total lost cause because nobody spoke Mandarin…So from then until the time we got shipped out of there in November, we just fooled around. The war had ended already and we thought we were going to go home, but they said, "No, you're going to go anyway." So they shipped the whole kit and caboodle of us over to China.

A war-torn country

They stuck us into an old Japanese hospital. It was the largest hospital, Japanese naval hospital on the China coast, as I was told. We were in little brick huts. It was pretty well run-down when we got there. The Japanese had sabotaged the whole compound. We went back in there and we fixed most of the damage…

The civilian population was very much down and out as far as food, and while we were eating, they would come by, beg for food as we were eating. And kids were coming by. As you dump your leftovers, they wouldn't let you dump it. They'd want to scrape it up and take it home. It was pretty pathetic. During the first day, it was pretty darn hard because all these kids were just roaming around your feet, asking for food.

[During a later assignment in Beijing], the civilians kind of looked at us and scratched their heads, and they would say, "They look like Chinese, but they can't

Dan Mar was commander of the American Legion Cathay Post #186 from 1952 to 1953.
—Courtesy of the American Legion Cathay Post #186.

be Chinese." And we looked at them, we smiled, we understood some of it, but not much, and we didn't really try to understand them or try to communicate with them too much because once you did, you'd get into the begging act. They would tell you that you're big military people and you come in here and you've got lots of money. You kind of get to the point eventually where you would stay away from them…Once in a while, if you have some change or something like that, you'd throw it to them. But you couldn't give money to all and you couldn't make even make a dent…then you get callous towards it a little later on.

I remember going through one of the parks in Beijing. We were in the Marine uniforms and this Chinese MP stopped us and he started speaking Chinese. They had a machine gun. There was a couple of them. They wanted to know where we were stationed at. Well, naturally, we weren't stationed there. So we just had to come out and show them: "Hey, you have no jurisdiction over us because we're U.S. military." And we show them our IDs and one of the guys said, "Now, go. Don't bother us." And the guys didn't bother us. Like I said, a lot of people just couldn't figure out our nationality or why, if we're Chinese, we were in American uniforms.

I wouldn't join the military again, but I wouldn't give it up for anything else. It was an experience. It was a positive experience as far as we were concerned. Sure, there was a war being fought and people getting killed and people were dying and starving and so on, but not being deep thinkers, I guess it didn't bother us.

Interviewed by Lily Eng and Sarah Vacatio.

American Legion Cathay Post #186 members celebrating the induction of their organization. Mar pictured far right, 1946.
—Courtesy of American Legion Cathay Post #186.

Frank MATSUDA

World War II
Army, 442nd Regimental Combat Team, 1943-1945
Technician 4th Grade

On Dec. 7, 1941, I was playing basketball in an empty lot where we all played. This was maybe around 10 o' clock and then around noon, a friend went back home. He came back after lunch and he said, "Geez, the Japs bombed Pearl Harbor." And I didn't know where that was or anything, so then I went back home and ate lunch and listened to the radio and sure enough, that's what I heard, all day long.

I don't recall my parents speaking about war or anything. I know when we were told to evacuate, my mom was scurrying around getting stuff to wear, clothing and things because the stuff we could bring to camp was what you could carry. The kids — all we had was a little suitcase. My mom had a great big bamboo thing — they used to call it koodi — and my dad had a suitcase. That's about all. Everything else we had to leave.

I knew we were going to go. I had a paper box and I had a big set of trains that I put in there and my stamp collection, coin collection and all my fishing gear and I had it in the corner of the basement, thinking no one would take all my possessions. And, of course, when I came back after the Army, I went down there and everything was gone.

[The family went to Camp Harmony in Puyallup, Wash., for evacuation]. When we went from Puyallup to Camp Minidoka, we went by train.

Combat is no pleasure. It's pretty scary and then you get down on the ground and that's when you start praying.

I remember that. We went by Mount Hood on the Oregon side. And next thing you know, we were in Idaho, out there in the desert. When we finally went to the campground, then you realized. We saw a guard tower, barbed wire and some of the soldiers there. We all went inside and then we were assigned a block where we were supposed to go.

We heard that they were asking for volunteers to work out in the sugar beets, so I signed up right away. After a while, I had enough of that so I decided to go back to camp. I met a friend again and he said, "Let's go to Salt Lake City." So I said sure; I didn't want to stay in the camp.

In Salt Lake City, we used to go to this café to eat, it was a Japanese café, and that's when I heard one of the waitresses say, "Did you know that the Army is accepting Japanese now?" And everybody was asking if that was true. After lunch, I went across east of Salt Lake City and there was Fort Douglas, Utah, and so I went up there and joined.

Overcoming bitterness

I didn't even know any of the Japanese Americans in internment camps refused to go, but I don't blame them at all. 'Cause sure, when I went to Puyallup or to Minidoka earlier, if they asked me to join the Army, I wouldn't have joined them. I was pretty bitter there for a while against the U.S. government. But after a while, it was okay, then I wanted to get on.

I didn't want to work there, working from paycheck to paycheck. And I didn't want to go back to camp. That's why I joined the Army.

During basic training at Camp Shelby, we heard a lot of boys who had friends overseas [in the 100th Battalion, all-Japanese Americans from Hawaii] say, "Oh, they are getting slaughtered." You knew guys were getting killed, but until you actually heard a gunshot or heard a shell or a bomb coming near you, it didn't really mean much.

The smell and sounds of battle

Combat is no pleasure. That's when you really get scared, especially when they're shooting at you. And if a bullet comes close to you, there's a big pop and you know it's really close to your head then. Otherwise, you just hear it zing. Then when the shell bursts from mortars, you'll never forget that burnt powder smell. And if you actually look and see what landed, you'll see a red flash and then black smoke. Dirt and rocks flying all over. It's pretty scary, and then you get down on the ground and that's when you start praying. Every once in a while, you hear a guy hollering for medic and you know somebody got hit.

One time, we were walking in the woods and on the ridge was a German patrol going by. Somebody shot. Everybody else started shooting so I started shooting. Whether I hit him or not, I don't know. We saw a lot of them up there. I'll tell you, I got sick. I couldn't eat for a couple days. When I saw the first dead German, he was lying in the ditch. He had a green uniform, and you could see the brown blood. This was summertime, all the flies and blood on his face and the flies were on it. He had a pale colored look. First time I saw a dead guy. We went a little farther and we saw a couple more in the ditch.

And the smell of a dead body – you never forget that, especially in the summertime. It's a vomiting smell. Like some of those Germans I saw, they died with their eyes open. Oh God, that was awful. That far away look but they're dead, you know. Flies all over their blood. That was awful. I couldn't eat all day.

I remember the Lost Battalion [a trapped Texas Ranger unit that was rescued by the 442nd]. After one mission, we were off the front lines and we went back maybe three or four miles. We were supposed to be able to take a shower. And then we had orders to pack up and get ready to move out. It was dark out already. They said something about a lost battalion and we had to be ready in five minutes. So what else could you do? I didn't get to take a bath. I was looking forward to that.

We all got on trucks and went up to the front line and got off. We marched all night and then in the morning, that's when we attacked. That's when everybody got up, started going from tree to tree, moving forward. Then these three machine guns just opened up on us. Guys were just dropping like flies.

This guy called Blondie from Hawaii, our sergeant, Yamashiro, and I were walking. Blondie was shot and it killed him and hit the sergeant. All I had was a bunch of holes in my sleeves; I didn't get hit that time. Blondie was groaning so I went over there. I couldn't do anything. I hollered for medic but he was too busy doing everybody else 'cause they were getting killed left and right. And so I was fairly close to his head and face and I couldn't do much. And he was crying for his mother, and geez, that was real bad.

And then we finally got to the Lost Battalion…in this little gully. And that's where those guys were staying. They had huts with logs on top of them. The Germans were just bombing them but they came out and this one guy was really happy to see us. We all gave him a cigarette and we all marched back out.

Interviewed by Ken Mochizuki.

Tatsuo N. MATSUDA

Korean War
5th Air Force, 15th and 49th Fighter Bomber Squadrons, 1952-1956
Airman 1st Class

During World War II, there were "I'm American-Chinese" buttons that came out to signify the difference between Chinese and Japanese. [Japanese Americans were classified "enemy aliens" and were under curfew and other restrictions.] I remember we had one Chinese family in the area who ran a restaurant. The kid's name was Buck Lee and I can remember him coming to school with an "I'm American-Chinese" button. I got his button. I wish I would've kept it.

I don't know whether it was the National Guard or whether it was the Army but they all came down [for the evacuation of Japanese Americans] with their bayonets and rifles. They thought we were going to do something and they were posting guards. We boarded an Army convoy truck.

We were related to the Shiga family. Hatch, one of the Shiga boys, was drafted right before the war started so he was in the service already. He came out to camp twice, once when he was going through intelligence school and then before shipping out overseas, he came out and visited us a second time. He came in uniform. I thought it was great.

Our Block 40, I think we had the most volunteers [for the 442nd Regimental Combat Team of Japanese Americans] in that camp. When they

left…you started thinking, "Gee, I would like to go too," but I was too young at 10 years old. If I was eligible, I would've gone. Later on in camp, some of those people who volunteered from our block died in the military. It kind of hit home. Heck, the more you wanted to get into service and go.

[After World War II, the family relocated to Kirkland. The military continued to draft young men.] At the time my draft notice came, I was very good friends with Shiro Kashino and that bunch [of local veterans from the 442nd]. Shiro would always tell me, "Don't go in the Army because you don't want to sleep in the mud holes. Join the Air Force; they sleep in nice barracks and stuff." So two of us, me and Bob Seckel, we volunteered to the Air Force.

At basic training, I was one of the short guys. For review parade, I always got left out, which was fine with me. They let all the tall guys go; it looked better than a little short guy walking in the back.

For me it was fun, I enjoyed it. I enjoyed the food. Nobody else would eat so I said, "Well hell, I might as well eat." I think because of my family training, you learn to eat everything. Everything on the table you ate. You can't be picky. So I enjoyed it. I started gaining weight!

Seeing segregation

After that, we went to Alabama. That's the first time I really saw segregation, the way it was down in the South. I remember the first time I got on the bus from

At basic training, I was one of the short guys. For review parade, I always got left out, which was fine with me.

base to the town. I'd get on the bus, I'd walk to the back, the bus don't start. Just sits there. So I'd just stay in the back and wonder what's going on and whether more customers are coming on the bus or what. And then, finally the bus driver comes back and says, "You're not supposed to be sitting back here." I said, "In Seattle, we always get on the bus and run to the back." He said, "No, you gotta sit up in front. Back is reserved for the Colored people." I said, "Oh. What am I?" He told me: "You Whitey, so you're supposed sit up in the front."

Working in the rear

I had orders to go overseas. And then during that time, the Korean conflict was going on. Overseas, I had a good time. I said never look at things negatively. I got to see a lot of the countries. And of course, being Air Force, you weren't really front line, but close to front line. We were support group. We guarded POWs (prisoners of war); they were mostly Koreans. We had them fill sandbags and things like that. When I was guarding them, there was an orchard of apples, these girls wanted those Korean apples, but we told them: "You gotta do this other stuff." One shift I was on, they started going toward the orchard. Once they got in the orchard, I wouldn't know where they were going to go. I had to yell, "Halt! Halt!" And I put a round in my rifle and they were still walking. So then I ordered what little Japanese words I could remember; I yelled "Tomare!" And they all stopped. And they all came back. I guess they all understood Japanese, because Japan must've ruled Korea for some time.

Another time, I was sitting in the outhouse, these two guys came in talking among themselves. "What the hell is a gook doing in our latrines?" I didn't say a dang thing; I just finished my job, put my pants on, and then I grabbed these two guys...I told him, "Hey, you guys better be careful who you talk about." "Oh, I didn't know you're one of us." I said, "Oh yeah, you're funny." There's always that feeling 'cause there are a lot of rednecks in the service; you're not going to get away from it.

Crazy things can happen

Me and the ambulance driver, we're sitting at the end of the runway and the plane was taking off and the pilot jettisoned his bombs. He couldn't get enough air speed to get up in the air so he jettisoned his bombs in order for him to lift off. And we're sitting on the end of the runway and I said, "Hey, there's a bomb coming down the runway. Let's get out of here!" But the driver froze. I couldn't get him out of the seat, so I just sat on top of him and drove the ambulance away. The bomb, of course, came rolling down the runaway and went off into the field someplace. But I told the driver, "Man, I'm not going to ride with you no more." But, you know, those funny things can happen in the service, so many crazy things can happen in the service. Of course, if we were in a war zone...it might've been a little different. Well, we were in a war zone, but our war zone was different from the front lines.

Interviewed by Pei Pei Sung and Craig Matsuda.

—Courtesy of Tatsuo "Nelson" Matsuda, 1952.

Kim MUROMOTO

World War II
Army, 442nd Infantry Regiment Combat Team, 1944-1946
Staff Sergeant

I got my draft notice about a year after the family was evacuated and sent to Tule Lake internment camp. So I went into the service in April 1944. Since I got called into the service, I thought, "Well, I better quit work and go back into camp and stay with my folks." I stayed with them for a little while until I was inducted.

We were hearing about a lot of war fatalities, especially about the 100th Battalion with Japanese Americans from Hawaii. Then after the first group of the 442nd [Regimental Combat Team of all Japanese Americans] was formed and they started going into combat, some reports were coming back that fellows from the camp were dying.

I had to do my duty. I said I was going to defend the country when I got out of camp, and that's what I had to do. I was hoping that my parents would get out of camp, by my being in the service.

Basic training was rough. Of course, they made a man out of you. The worst was that 15 mile hike with a pack. You almost died by the time you got back. They trained us pretty fast 'cause they wanted to get us overseas to replace the ones who were gone.

[While preparing to go into war], the only thing that I really recall thinking was, "Boy, I wonder what my parents would do in camp if I was – if I didn't come back." That was the only really bad thought that I had

before I left: What are my folks were going to do if I don't come back?

I joined the 442nd in the latter part of October – just missed the rescue of the Lost Battalion [Texas Rangers who were trapped by Germans] by just a few days. When members of the 442nd came back, there were only a few men left on each company. They didn't say too much. Of course, they wouldn't – they were all in more or less aftershock. The company that I got into, I think there were less than a dozen men left from that company. They were really devastated because they lost so many friends. We left right away from there.

Taking the Gothic Line

In March, Gen. Mark Clark wanted his 442 back, so we were secretly sent back down there by boat. We landed in Italy. Early one morning, we took off from there and climbed the hill [called the Gothic Line] where the Germans had held off the Allies through the winter months. It was real steep. In fact, we had to zigzag back and forth, 'cause it was really steep. It was night time, so I really couldn't tell, but I know there was one fellow who did slip and fall and rolled down maybe about 100 feet or so. They said, "Boys, don't let out any yells or anything like that." So I guess when he fell, boy, he didn't say a word. He just rolled and rolled and rolled.

You didn't hang on to any guy. You were a little bit behind him but you knew you were following. You could still see the guy ahead of you; it wasn't really that pitch dark but it was

I think it was June of '46 when our group brought the regimental colors back and we went to Washington D.C., and paraded in front of President Truman.

hard to see, until you got up to the top and you can see the daylight kind of breaking. But then the Germans were on top of that hill and they started firing machine guns and we kind of ducked under the boulders to protect ourselves.

Luckily, we were the first ones to get up to the top. Two companies got up to the top…but there was one company that was still back down in the town. When we got up there, we surprised the Germans. Then they started shelling down at the town and some guys got killed or hurt in that one company that stayed back. It was day by that time. We could see a machine gun nest up in the top…but then we started throwing mortars up there and captured the hill so the Germans started retreating from there.

It was scary, especially when the artillery came in on you, that's when it was really scary. But, of course, when you saw your first fatality too — that's the scariest. One of my buddies, the guy right next to me got killed when we were going up one hill — this was a little bit later on. I called for the medic but he was hit earlier, so I had to try and patch him up myself. I knew it was no use 'cause he had a gunshot hit to the lungs, in the stomach and down in the leg. That was the worst experience; you just hate to see anybody go like that.

I remember this one night, I think I had the 11 p.m. – 1 a.m. shift and this one fellow from Hawaii sat up with me and we talked and talked and talked. And finally it was time for me to go back into my foxhole and he went back into his foxhole. And there was this one new recruit that came in the middle of the night and joined him in his foxhole, and that night we caught a big barrage. The both of them got killed, got tree burst and came right down on them. Luckily, we had built our foxhole into the wall, so my partner and I lucked out. We must have lost about eight men that night. I think maybe some rocks may have come down from the top of our foxhole and hit me on the head or some-thing 'cause I don't remember a thing. My partner told me later, "You were sleeping so good, and I put my ear up to your nose and you were breathing so I figured you were all right so I just let you sleep."

When you see a fellow soldier get killed, lot of times you just think, well we've got to go sooner or later and you feel sorry for the fellow and you feel sorry for the family. You have to continue on and hope that you don't fall into the same fate. You can't think of it any other way, I guess. Can't sit there and cry about it 'cause it's your life or the other guy's life. So you keep going.

At first, we had just entered Poe Valley. Then word comes down from head-quarters that the war has ended. Then you didn't do anymore fighting. The Germans were all retreating and getting rounded up there anyway. We felt great, great that it's over. I mean, you're so fatigued, you're so tired and everything — and naturally, you're glad that it was over. But you didn't go out to celebrate or anything like that.

I think it was June of '46 when our group brought the regimental colors back and we went to Washington, D.C., and paraded in front of President Truman. I think there was about 500 of us. And we received the 7th Presidential Unit Citation. They were all hakujins (Caucasians) cheering. The only thing that I could remember was that I was really proud to be there.

Interviewed by Ken Mochizuki.

Kim Muromoto, (far left), and members of 442nd Regimental Combat Team help keep each other's moral up during difficult times, 1944.
—Courtesy of Kim Muromoto.

Mike MUROMOTO

Vietnam War
Air Force, 315th Air Commando Squadron, 1965-1971
Sergeant

My dad, Kim, was in the 442nd Regimental Combat Team. I felt I had to serve. I was proud to serve. My dad served, my uncles served. So I'm thinking, "It's my duty as an American." I never thought of it as "I'm-going-to-beat-the-draft" type thing, but I did start looking at it and thought, "Fine. Let's not get stupid about it either. I'll do my job in the service, but let's not go in as a foot soldier."

I went into the Air Force. I went to Fort Benning, Ga., for jump school. I learned how to jump out of airplanes and rappel off 60-foot towers. I said, "There's something wrong with this picture. Air Force people aren't supposed to be jumping out of airplanes; they're supposed to ride in them. We're suppose to have it nice, sit back 40 miles away from the fighting."

Racism and stereotypes

The American South was kind of different. It was a culture shock for me. I went to these outlying towns and saw signs that said White and Colored. I would look at these two signs and try to figure out which bathroom, which drinking fountain to use. I felt that I was stuck right in the middle because both the Blacks and Mexicans were in a separate class structure in the South. I was an outsider.

When the door of the airplane opened, my stomach just fell right to the ground because I realized that the war was real and I was in it.

I felt that the military itself stereotyped me. They expected me to succeed. I was Japanese. I was Oriental. They expected me to score high on any aptitude test. I was supposed to be in the 80 to 90 percentile range because I was Japanese.

'This is not what war is supposed to be.'

My unit knew we were going overseas because all of a sudden, we're getting these funny camouflage uniforms and other units are being issued green fatigues and khakis. I was 22 years old and in charge of seven people when we landed in Vietnam. When the door of the airplane opened, my stomach just fell right to the ground because I realized that the war was real and I was in it. I thought, "Now I'm in combat and my decisions make or break the team. We're either going to come back or we're going to die."

The first thing I noticed was... at the airport, they had a Vietnamese woman come by every half-hour to clean out the toilets for the foreigners. The Vietnamese themselves were using the field next to the runway as a bathroom. I was embarrassed because they were Oriental, just like me.

At Tan Son Nhut Air Base, a group of us were walking around the base in civilian clothes when I heard an Army GI say, "There's another gook. Get him out of our way." They then bumped into me and I turned around and looked at them. I said, "What did you say?" This poor guy turned beet red. I told him: "Corporal, you had better watch your mouth." That's the first time I ever got mad because of name-calling. This guy called me a gook; I had never been called that before.

My first firefight was near Highway 13, in III Corps. My team was sent there to set up a LZ (landing zone) for the 1st Division. We got our equipment set up then holy hell broke loose. I heard machine gunfire…and stuff like that. All of a sudden here comes big stuff, mortars and heavy artillery fire. It scared the hell out of me; I wasn't sure what to do. Everything seemed to be spinning in my head, when my RTO (radio operator) hollered at me, saying, "Where do you want the perimeter set up?" I came to my senses and got the perimeter set up. The team survived, no thanks to me.

The first Vietnamese POWs (prisoners of war) I saw were Vietcong. These scrawny 80-120 pound men/boys are doing this much damage to us? One POW had to be 60 years old if not older. Another was a kid maybe 12 or 13. We captured females too, packing weapons and ammo. It really surprised me. You're thinking, "Okay, I'm 22. I should be fighting someone 18 to maybe 40, but not 12 to 60." I had never heard of Vietnam, let alone understood its history. After you learn some of the history, you see a different picture. These people had been fighting all their lives. You go to Vietnam, full of patriotism, and you have all these old and young guerrillas fighting against you, believing in their cause. This is not what the war was supposed to be. You're supposed to go in there and shoot somebody in a different colored uniform. Now you're going in there and you don't know who the enemy is.

No welcome home

We never knew what was going on stateside except who won the Miss America Pageant or the World Series. I didn't know there was protesting going on. Some of the new guys would tell you: "There are a bunch of hippie college students protesting the war." We didn't know or understand the extent of what was happening. That's why we were never worried about it, until we got off the plane at Travis AFB (Air Force Base) and went to San Francisco to catch a flight to Seattle. At the airport, there were a bunch of long-haired freaks. There were five of us. They saw us coming. We were in uniform. All we wanted to do was to get our tickets and go home. These hippies started yelling at us and that was it. Knock-down, drag-out fight, right there in the San Francisco airport.

We fought a war for our country and when we got home we were chastised for doing what our country wanted us to do. My dad asked why I was so bitter and standoffish to everybody. I said, "When you came back from the European Theater, your family was behind barbed wire. But the 442nd received recognition and got a parade. I came back from combat; all I got was a fight. That's the difference." We were never recognized. When I got back from Vietnam, the Nisei Vets Committee never asked me to join. They never said thank you to me. I'm Japanese American. I fought in Vietnam. I still carry shrapnel in my body. About 10 years ago they asked me to join. They didn't want me when I first got back, now they want me to join? I don't think so.

Lasting impacts

When I got back from Vietnam, it was real hard for me. Seeing Asians back here in the States reminded me of Vietnam. I had this gut hatred…for the Vietnamese. Don't get me wrong. There are good Vietnamese and bad, just like any nationality, race or creed. But, after what I went through over there, it is hard to associate with other Asians. I felt comfortable over on the White side again because that's who I worked with, that's who I fought with. Except for the few Asians who were in the service, the Asians I saw were either the enemies or the Vietnamese. And coming back stateside, I didn't want anything to do with them. I didn't want to remember the war. So I went back to my cars and tried not to remember. It has taken a long time for me to get over my bitterness toward the Vietnamese. For me, as a Japanese American, I should have known better. I remember how some people treated me. And I treated the Vietnamese the same way. I guess time heals all, or maybe it is maturity.

Interviewed by Ken Mochizuki and Firia Aguon.

Richard H. NAITO

World War II
Army, 442nd Regimental Combat Team, 1943-1946
Private 1st Class

When World War II broke out and they started speaking of evacuating people with Japanese ancestry, that was certainly a shock and disappointment. When I went to school, I was taught that I was an American, just as good as Caucasian scholars. And starting out with that and then being evacuated – I couldn't believe it. It was just like a dream. After getting evacuated, there was no other choice {but to volunteer for the military}. I had to prove that I'm American, good American and go to fight for my country.

While in the Camp Minidoka concentration camp, I volunteered for a work group and served as general manager of warehouses, transportation and supply. In 1942, I searched for any sort of employment, but businesses wouldn't hire any person of Japanese descent. I polished cars for a while and thought, "This is no good. I've got to volunteer." So I volunteered myself out of Spokane.

When I went to the enlistment office, they said, "Well, great. This is what we want: more people like you." I said, "Don't get excited. I don't know whether you can even accept me, yet." And they didn't take me in right away. I had to wait. Then they finally asked me to report to Camp Shelby, Miss., to be part of the original 442nd. When I volunteered, I was 31.

You fight for your country, get wounded and lie in a hospital, then the military organization turns you down?

When I volunteered, I didn't know of the No-No Boys [interned Japanese Americans who refused to volunteer for the military. The nickname came from their answers to questions about their loyalty to the United States and their willingness to join the U.S. military]. I heard about it in Camp Shelby after I was in the service. At the time, I didn't go for that. I was mad. Supposedly everybody said, "No, I won't bear arms against the mother country." I thought that was wrong but after thinking it over, we'd been fighting exactly for what they were doing. I didn't quite understand that completely back then. I've been reading up on that; they were fighting for their rights. We were fighting physically to give them that right.

Reality of war

If you're not scared about combat, you're either so religious that you figure God is going to take care of you or something, but if you're normal, you've got to be afraid. There's nothing as scary as war, especially when the artillery is pouring in.

When I got hit, it was the third little village that we were taking in Italy. We thought that, well, we'd taken two of them. We thought it'd be a cinch and it wasn't. I got hit and I got pinned down with two friends…We got behind a stalk of wheat and every time we tried to move, the machine guns poured in. I think I got hit about two o'clock in the afternoon, and resistance was so tough that our forces pulled back and poured artillery in. There was no medic, of course, because they pulled back. My wounds hurt like mad and I thought, "Gee, I wish one of the shells would hit me." And this was July and it had become dark overhead. Somebody said,

"Hey, Dick." I thought, "My, I've heard from heaven." And then they picked me up on a stretcher. They dumped me again because they opened machine gunfire, and then finally got me out.

I woke up in a field evac, which was a tent and the bottom was all grass. They moved me from hospital to hospital. Then by hospital ship, they shipped me back to New York. And by then, I had hepatitis and discoloration. The guys who were in the hospital ship were able to see the Statue of Liberty. "Come on, Dick. Come on, Dick. The Statue of Liberty," they said. And I was feeling real bad by then and I didn't get up. I was there five days and then they put me on a train through a window. When I reached Spokane, it was about two or three in the morning. They put me out through a window again. Both legs were in full-blown casts. Twenty-one months, I stayed there.

When I first got to Spokane Baxter General Hospital, they didn't say it directly to me…but the nurse…told me that the Caucasian soldiers in the hospital said, "I'm going to get that Jap." Naturally, all the wounded in Spokane fought in the Pacific against the Japanese so when they saw someone like me, they're going to get him. The nurse told the guys, "What country's uniform do you think he wore?" That kept them off my back. Later, we became friends.

Rejection by Veterans of Foreign Wars

During that time we were recovering, one of the Caucasian soldiers asked me, "Would you like to join VFW (Veterans of Foreign Wars)?" And I said yeah, so he put my name in. I got turned down.

I thought, "What is this? I offer my life to fight for our country. I come back wounded and they don't want to accept me again?" You fight for your country, get wounded, lie in the hospital, and then the military organization turns you down? Not until 1997, one VFW member asked, "Would you accept a life membership and we'll pay for it?" I said, "Sure, I'll accept it." Otherwise, I would practice the same thing, reverse discrimination, and where's that going to get you?

One other experience I had while in Baxter General Hospital in Spokane: The chaplain came to me and asked me if I could interview a Japanese prisoner. I told the chaplain: "I'm not very good at Japanese, but I'll try." He was a prisoner but he was wounded. He got wounded in Alaska and I didn't even know that the Japanese had gotten into Alaska. He looked very young. As a matter of fact, I thought if he was 18, he'd be lucky. I only asked what the chaplain

asked me to ask him. I kind of felt sorry for him – so young. I was 31 at that time. This man was young and he hadn't seen his family for years. He was wounded and, if anything, I had compassion for him. He was doing the same thing that I was doing; he was fighting for his country.

War isn't all bad. There are times to laugh. I believe in fate. I didn't think I would come back, go into war and come back. And here I am back. And I know people who went through the whole war and never got wounded, and to me, that's exceptional…The United States of America has never seen war. She has a people who have never experienced what war is like. You either kill or get killed. And that's war. If there is such a thing as living hell, war is. And I wouldn't wish that on nobody. As far as fighting for our country, I'm very proud that I did it. If I was younger and the time of war came, I would do the same thing. But I sure wouldn't volunteer for combat infantry.

Interviewed by Linda Ando and Tammy Lu.

—Courtesy of Richard H. Naito, 1943.

Bill NISHIMURA

World War II
Military Intelligence Service, 317th Troop Carrier Wing, 1944-1946
Staff Sergeant

The war had ended as we were going across the Pacific, but we didn't know if there would be stray Japanese submarines, so we took a zigzag course. From Los Angeles, it took us 30 days to get to the Philippines. We stopped off at the Marshall Islands and onto the Philippines. Out of 2,000 GIs aboard the ship, there were 500 of us Nisei [second generation Japanese American] soldiers. My first impression of Manila – it's bombed out...and the huge Army trucks would come...and they were all dusty and dirty and muddy...I was used to seeing polished Army trucks in the states, even when we were in the training camp. Military Intelligence Service soldiers would leave the vessel, the cargo nest...and get onto the trucks heading towards our encampment. The natives would see us; they're yelling: "Tomodachi, tomodachi!" What the hell's going on here, I thought. Then I realized that this area was occupied for a couple years by the Japanese troops. The natives assumed we were from Japan even though we were wearing GI outfits.

While we were in the Philippines, 500 of us were in this camp, a former race track...outside of Manila. We were waiting for assignments. What we were sent over for was the big invasion of Japan. This is why we were rushed over, but the war had ended. So we were waiting for assignments to whatever outfit needed interpreters or translators. Some got sent to the POW (prisoner of war) camp right outside of northern Luzon and the rest of us were still in camp waiting.

The aftermath of war

After a few months in the Philippines, the Nisei soldiers who were still unassigned got shipped to Yokohama. I got assigned to the United States strategic bombing survey team. We conducted two interviews per day and each interview took at least two hours. We worked from Tokyo all the way down to Hiroshima to conduct interviews. It has been over 50 years, but I do remember some of the questions we asked during the two-hour interview. We started off by asking if they were able to get enough food, how was their health. We asked, "What do you miss most as far as food supplies is concerned?" Then, after a series of casual questions, we moved on to a series of meatier questions such as, "During the air raids, what type of bombs did you fear the most, the incendiary or the explosive type?" The same questions were asked from Tokyo, Okayama, Ebara and on down. And then, when we got to Kure...outside of Hiroshima, we asked the same set of questions. We also asked, "Were you aware of any propaganda leaflets? What kind of leaflets?" Although Hiroshima was not on our itinerary, we made a special trip to

When we got to Hiroshima, not one child asked us for anything. That's when we opened our hearts and our pockets for them. We felt so sorry for them.

that city. It was just a matter of months since the atom bomb was dropped. At that time, they had our MPs (military police) surrounding the city limits. Only authorized personnel were able to enter. We were authorized to enter because we were with the special bomb team. It was so depressing to us Niseis, especially seeing the scarred children walking silently and aimlessly around the ruins. There were seven of us on the team and two Caucasians. We're doing all the work, but they were the officers – that's the way it went. I remember one Caucasian fellow who had a coke bottle, the size of a tape cassette container; it melted. Can you imagine how radioactive it is? But we didn't know that. The coke bottle had flattened to the size of a tape container. And he said, "Look at the souvenir I got." We didn't even think of picking up souvenirs; why would we? We felt so sad for the kids. All the way down from Tokyo, whatever village or city we'd go to, little kids would ask for chewing gum or chocolate and we'd be free with it…pass it out. When we got to Hiroshima, not one child asked us for anything. That's when we opened our hearts and our pockets for them. We felt so sorry for them. Who would even think of picking up a souvenir, under such circumstances?

Later on, I was stationed in Tachikawa Air Base after I went back to the NYK office building and flew around Tokyo. I saw how flat Tokyo was, but that was the result of thousands of bombs. But in Hiroshima, which is a bigger city than Seattle…with a couple million people, one bomb did the same thing. When you see something like that, you think, "Oh my Lord, I wish there would never be another war." You honestly think that. Like recently, President Bill Clinton was threatening to have an air raid on Iraq, and I was praying to God it wouldn't happen. I would rather have world leaders discuss it over a table and hammer…out a peaceful solution. I'm sure there must be a peaceful way to resolve all these differences.

Lasting bonds

The MIS had a 50th reunion around three years ago. I dug around and got a list of 10 people who took basic training with me in Fort McClellan, Ala., and who slept together in these 12-man tents in the Philippines…During this reunion, I told them that one evening we would have a mini-reunion at our place. We did that and we had a marvelous time; they still talk about it. Don't hear from them anymore, but a couple of them, we still communicate. We hadn't seen each other for over 50 years. It was really something.

When the Nisei vets came back to Seattle, we had a choice of either joining the American Legion or the VFW (Veterans of Foreign Wars). If you hook on with a national organization, you have to give a portion of your membership dues to the mother organization. A handful of fellows said, "Why not get together and make our own veterans group? Call it Nisei Veteran Club, Nisei Veterans Committee." There was an old kendo hall…we bought for $1,000. Two or three times a week, we'd go there and fix it up. We sanded the gym floor. We put the new siding on and repainted it and we made all the benches. Lefty Ichihara was the straw boss. He didn't believe in buying anything. He'd make a template and he'd buy the legs and we'd make the darn thing. So all the benches we used for Memorial Day, those were benches we made. But the ranks are getting thin, so now we're wondering, "Who's going to take over?"

Interviewed by Charlene Mano and Pei Pei Sung.

Mack NOGAKI (1912-1999)

World War II
Army, 442nd Regimental Combat Team, 232nd Combat Engineers,
1943-1946
Technician 5th Grade

When I heard about Pearl Harbor, I was home in Seattle. I was going to see some girls at Bainbridge Island. While I was going over there, a man came up to me and said, "That was a pretty terrible thing, wasn't it?...It's going to be real tough on you guys. I know because my father was a German during the first World War and they were very badly treated. You guys stand out more and so you're going to get it worse." I said, "No, I'm an American citizen." He said, "That doesn't make any difference." And he was right.

I was working at Eatonville and they said, "You're going to be interned." I just couldn't believe it. But I came back to Seattle, there were these signs on the telephone poles [ordering restrictions for people of Japanese ancestry]. There was a curfew. I still couldn't take it and so I said, "To hell with it." I would go out every night and never obey the curfew law. I just walked and every time there was a policeman, I looked him right in the eye and he didn't do anything.

[While in Camp Harmony in Puyallup, Wash.], I remember this Chinese guy used to come. He was a restaurant man in Seattle. One time he came to see us at the gate and he had a big cake. The guard came up,

We heard they wanted us in a combat team and there was quite a murmur. "Hey! We're off with this suicide squad, right?

—Photo reprinted with permission by the Seattle Post-Intelligencer, 1994.

"What you got there?" He said, "I got a cake. Give it to my friends." And the guard said, "Give me that cake" and he took out his bayonet and shoved it in there, all over the cake. Punched it full of holes. And that Chinese guy got so mad. I was afraid that he was going to hit that guy and here these guys are armed guards. He cussed that guy out. I could never forget that. And he just stood there and cussed those soldiers out.

Miss Mahon came one time. She was the principal of Bailey Gatzert school. She was standing outside of this gate, and she was just running back and forth. She said, "I taught you wrong! I never thought this would happen!" And she was crying there.

At Camp Minidoka, it was just the feeling that you were in prison, the fact that there were guards standing out there. This thing would always gnaw on you. We were not criminals...

We went to this discussion. There were four guys who were already in the Army. They came and tried to talk us into going in, but most of the talking was done by some second lieutenant. He said, "I promise you that if you guys come out and fight in the Army, they will never question you're American." We heard they wanted us in a combat team and there was quite a murmur. "Hey! We're off with this suicide squad, right?"

I said, "To hell with it. You guys throw us in the camps and now want to put us in the front line. You can shove it." And I left the meeting. Then I got home and I thought about it and I thought about it and said, "No other way. You gotta go." So the next morning, some of the guys...signed right there. I left but the next day, I went and volunteered.

At boot camp, they took me out and put me in the engineers because I was a crane operator at the Eatonville sawmill. We would go in to do this engineer's work, which was mostly support, taking care of the roads so that the supplies can come through. There were all kinds of work that we had to do, like keeping the trails right, and also we had to handle all the explosives, which was the dirtiest work in the bunch. We lost almost as many men to explosions as we did from enemy rifle fire. I don't have the exact number of explosions, but we did have one explosion where we lost three men. During the early part of the war, they were having a demonstration to the infantry on what to expect with explosives. Somebody made a mistake and this truck loaded with mines blew up. Killed five men. And three of them were men from our company.

Discrimination even after the war

After the war, I stopped in New Jersey where my brother had relocated. And then my sister was working in Washington, D.C., so I spent about three, four days there…then I came home to Seattle. When I came back, I didn't know what I was going to do. I went back to Eatonville to get my job back there. The foreman said, "We'd rather you not come back because if you come back, all the Japanese would come back. You're all right, but you know" – this kind of attitude.

They asked me to come the union meeting [of sawmill workers]. I told them, "You guys think you're good Americans. I think I'm a good American too because, hey, I was in the front lines fighting for you guys. Maybe we needed you guys to back us up, but I was in the front line. I volunteered for service. And now you guys won't even give me my job back. You can keep your old job." I walked out of that meeting.

I came back to Seattle. I didn't have a job. I didn't know what to do. My sisters and brothers were always looking out, "Hey, I got a nice job dishwashing over here." I said, "I didn't go to the Army just to come back to be a dishwasher."

Then I was walking along Lake Union and I saw a big "shipbuilders wanted" sign. I went in there and saw the guy and I said, "I just come out of the service and I like to get a job." He said, "I have a little problem here with the union and we don't know if we can take you on, but if the union says it's all right, we'll take you." I went up to the union office and was told, "No, you can't go to work there." I said, "Why not? Why can't I go?" He says, "Cool it, cool it." This one guy came up and was grumbling. I said, "What are you grumbling about?" He said, "Well you guys come in here, and you don't know a damn thing and then you get the same wages as I do and I been working for so long. I don't think that's fair." I said, "I think I can learn. I went into the Army and I fought. You guys come back and make a lot of overtime because of the work, 'cause you had to support us…If I could become a good enough soldier to win the war, hey, I could learn to be a shipbuilder." He said, "That's right. Okay." And then he apologized for it.

Interviewed by Debbie Kashino McQuilken, courtesy of Seattle Sansei.

Katashi OITA

World War II
Military Intelligence Service, 163rd Language Detachment, 1944-1946
Technician 3rd Grade

I spent about three months in internment camp and I was drafted. I went to the Army in Fort Douglas in Utah and by then, I was already accepted to go to Fort Snelling as a Japanese language specialist. We went overseas but by then the actual fighting was over. It wasn't official peace so we were aboard a troop ship. I was thinking, "Gee, I hope all the submarines know that the war is over." We ended up in Manila, that's where the Airline Translation Interpretation Section was located... and we were attached to Gen. Douglas MacArthur's GHQ (General Headquarters). I don't remember doing much of anything there, though what I do remember about the place is that every afternoon, from about two to four o'clock, it rained. So we always used to wait for the rain to take a shower. That's some muddy water.

We would be in groups getting ready for invasion in Japan, which never happened. In September, finally we went to Japan for occupation duty. We went to Tokyo and...to the NYK building, the Newport Youth and Kaisha, the shipping company building. I think about that place and I remember I never had such good food in all my Army life.

In November, I was sent to Hiroshima prefecture. I was...in that area right after the atomic bomb so I saw what the atomic bomb caused at that time. I had seen other bombed cities like Manila and all these places, but Manila, you saw grasses growing and flies and everything. But when I went to Hiroshima, it was really dead; there's nothing alive. The people of Hiroshima were having problems. They were trying to stay alive, but they certainly didn't give us any trouble.

The feeling I get is most of the younger generation doesn't realize what war is. The 442nd Regiment and the 100th Battalion [of all Japanese Americans] – they were the ones who really made the reputation for the Niseis [second generation Japanese Americans], and, in fact, I think they did it for all the Asians. But in the case of the Army, they almost expect too much of us. After all, the number one man in the whole U.S. Army [the chief of staff] is a Japanese American, Gen. Eric Shinseki. In the period of 50 years, we came from a group that was segregated and it was hard to become an officer...to the point where we are the number one in the U.S. That's an amazing thing.

Interviewed by Pei Pei Sung.

The feeling I get is most of the younger generation doesn't realize what war is. The 442nd and the 100th made the reputation...for all Asians.

JoAnn L. OLIGARIO

Vietnam War
Navy Hospital Corps, Operating Room Section, 1965-1968
E-4

I grew up on a strawberry farm on Bainbridge Island and went to high school in the early 1960s. It was a time in our country when there wasn't a lot of respect for diversity and no EEOC (Equal Employment Opportunity Commission) oversaw or helped to correct injustices. It was very difficult for Filipino or Native kids. We all suffered a lot prejudice.

We didn't really have the money for college and I think I wanted to escape some of the problems on Bainbridge. I thought it would be good for me to go into the Navy. I'll travel and get an education. Something about going into the military intrigued me, I guess. I thought it would be a good career, was going to probably do it for 20 years. But I didn't know, when I went in, what the Vietnam War was all about. You go in, you're 18…you have no idea. I went when the war was very escalated and I found that out when I was at Great Lake Naval Hospital 'cause a lot of the…Marines were being sent over earlier and earlier to Vietnam.

I was looked upon as an equal, treated as an equal. Boot camp…it was kind of fun because we had a co-ed company. There was a wonderful group of people. You established a second family really quick in the service. We were really close and it was very hard for us to leave Illinois. A lot of…the boys were going directly to Marine units.

I feel really thankful about the service because it helped me grow up in a lot of different ways. It established a lot of my anti-war feelings.

Seeing the horrors of war stateside

From Great Lakes Naval Hospital, I went on to Philadelphia Naval Hospital to become an operating room technician in 1966. My first day there at the naval hospital…gave me a little bit of an idea of what Vietnam was all about. This naval hospital had a huge psychiatry ward there, some were locked wards. A patient somehow got out of a confined ward. He went to one of the buildings of the hospital and jumped off to commit suicide. They didn't have the word post-traumatic stress syndrome back then.

I was a pretty sheltered farm girl. My family and I never really discussed things about war. And, I think, the majority of the young people who went into the service didn't know either. My very first case in the operating room was a leg amputation. A young man who recently returned from Vietnam was going to have his leg amputated. When the orthopedic surgeon handed me his leg, I had to make my feelings numb to continue. I knew what it was going to be all about then. He was so young. He was probably not much older than I was…

Philadelphia Naval Hospital was a big rehab center also for prosthetics. It was not uncommon to see groups of five to eight young men amputated below the knee, about the knee, one leg, both legs. I would think they were a good support system for each other, but what happens when they go home?

There was a fellow who died in intensive care. We had done some surgery on him and I had talked with him a little bit. They had done some extensive surgery on his belly and his wife came and she was pregnant. He had a lot of abdominal injury and wounds into the chest too. I think it was a claymore mine injury, the bombs that took a lot of the guys' legs off. I would go over there to talk with him and his wife…because he was a farm boy also. I think he was from the Midwest. We would talk about everything besides hospital work. We would talk about farm life, getting the chicken and eggs in the morning, walking cows and it was my way to kind of touch base with somebody who…grew up the same way I did. His wife was really nice. I was really kind of heartbroken. He didn't survive and she was pregnant. I went over to see him and he was gone.

I was just very upset about the war. My being upset didn't assess judgment. I was very upset about how horribly injured people were and how, psychologically, people were injured also. It didn't all come into place; it was a gradual thing. Then when I started losing friends, I started getting really upset, getting angry. So many young men and I thought that they were used as pawns.

A civilian friend would keep more in touch with some of the men who went to Vietnam. In our personnel office, on the second floor, he would post an informal list of people he learned were killed in Vietnam. I wouldn't go up to the second floor. Once, I had to go talk to the administrative officer on that floor. Someone who I had…known not even two months beforehand was on the list. He had gone over to Vietnam and I don't know the circumstance of his death. The thing is you didn't know the circumstances about how a lot of them died. Well, you got that funny feeling in your stomach and you just kind of felt numb. I think you still feel it today.

Reflections on war

I feel really thankful about the service 'cause it helped me grow up in a lot of different ways. It established a lot of my anti-war feelings. I think war is terrible, a lot of it is so unnecessary. There's profit from war and that's one of the things that I'm just really against, the Dow Chemical Company or the people who make munitions. I mean there's a responsibility about war that needs to be followed up afterwards. You have to go back to that community, to Vietnam, Cambodia or wherever because there's a lot of people who got maimed from that war. They need to be helped…to reestablish their community, their homes. We must go back and help remedy some things so they can survive.

I've put off going to the Vietnam Veterans Memorial because I still deal with grief…today. I guess it's just my own form of post-traumatic stress syndrome. You still feel numbness. You still feel achy mentally, not only for the people in the service who went through all those atrocities, but I feel the grief…for the people in Vietnam, in Cambodia.

Interviewed by Lily Eng and Sarah Vacatio.

JoAnn L. Oligaria begins her tour at Great Lakes Naval Hospital the summer of 1965.
—Courtesy of JoAnn L. Oligario.

Kaun ONODERA

World War II
Army, 442nd Regimental Combat Team, 1943-1946
Private 1st Class

My younger brother, Satoru (Sat), had been working on Sand Point Naval station as a laborer at the time Pearl Harbor broke out. He was canned. Ko, my older brother, was working as a laborer down at the terminal station on King Street and he was laid off immediately after Pearl Harbor. The next day…he went down and tried to join the Marines. They turned him down. Sat tried to join the Navy. I was working downtown for Bartell Drugs. I had worked for them for about six years since 1936. They didn't fire me but they fired a lot of other Japanese employees who worked for Bartell.

[Once the military allowed Japanese Americans back in the military], the three of us brothers volunteered at the same time out at concentration camp – each not knowing that the others were going to volunteer. Each of us independently thought, "I should go." We were just kind of shocked when we all three came home from that one day.

Since the three of us separately did that, there was something there in terms of family and cultural and ethnic honor or loyalty – whatever you want to call it. If we were in Japan and they had asked for volunteers for the Japanese Army, we might have volunteered 'cause that's our idea of loyalty, of service.

The three of us brothers volunteered at the same time out of concentration camp – each not knowing that the others were going to volunteer.

Saturo, Ko and Kaun Onodera, 1943.
—Courtesy of Onodera Family

I remembered very vaguely [the loyalty questionnaire that interned Japanese Americans had to sign]. I was asked if I was going to volunteer, I said "yes," and that's all there was to it. The questionnaire said: "Do you swear all loyalty…" and that had to be a yes. And, yes, I was willing to serve in the military of the U.S.A. That's what they meant by the yes-yes. But I never thought too much about that; all I knew was that I came in to volunteer as soon as I had heard about it.

My father would go up to talk in Japanese about the righteousness of volunteering, of proving yourself an American and that this was our country. Whether we were citizens or not, this was our country. Regardless of how we had been treated, this is where we would live and die.

German POWs treated better

We were through basic training in a couple of months but they shipped us for some crazy duty. We went down and guarded all the German prisoners from North Africa for a peanut harvest down in Alabama. We'd go to Ft. McClellan, pick up these German prisoners…who were the pick of Aryan watch. We'd have these trucks, loaded with these handsome German soldiers…and here were these slant-eyed Orientals, a couple on each side and one at the end with their rifles. The truck would go through industrial parts of Alabama that only employed women. So all these women, they'd come out of their factories. Man, they'd rave about the German soldiers 'cause there were no men around; they're either working on farm or defense. That's what I'd say was rather ironic: They were cheering them, not us.

And here's the other part: We'd get to a farm and we'd put the prisoners in the field. They'd go about working all right and not knocking themselves out. This is mid-October, still hot down south, muggy hot. We had rations of two peanut butter sandwiches and a canteen of water…for the whole day…The farmer would come out about 10:30 in the morning carrying cases of…ice-cold Coke, boiled eggs, raw bacon and loaves of bread and that's the prisoners' morning snack. We didn't get shit! What kind of war is this?

The responsibilities of leadership

I didn't ever want to be an officer. Maybe I did act in some leadership situation in the service but I never aspired to it. I'd just as soon be a everyday buck private, be one of the gang. There was a hell of a lot of responsibility. It's not that one avoided the responsibility; it's just that you could see that it'd be a tough thing if you were the head of a squad. You'd assign somebody to this job, and you'd assign somebody else to this position and, of course, it was your decision-making that resulted…in who got killed, wounded or whatnot. You'd kind of feel responsible or guilty about it, at least that's the way I looked at it anyway.

Something came up in the headquarters platoon where the captain took a fancy to me because he found out I had been a clerk…He pulled me in as a supply sergeant and an assistant to his assistant. It was a scary job at times. I remember one dark night when all hell was breaking loose all around us. We were up in the FO (frontal offensive) position and he told me, "Hey Kaun, I want you to go back to company headquarters and get me some cigarettes. I'm all out of cigarettes." It was a hell of a way back down the hill in the dark…They had firepower coming over and everything else in the dark too. Heck, I must have come down there like superman, jumping all over. They used to give us rations all the time – no Camels or Lucky's at that time. Chelseas – that was the best I could get. Back I went up that mountainside again, up to the captain…and I gave him the cigarettes. He said, "As of tonight, your going to be private 1st class." I got one stripe after that.

Just before we went up to rescue the Lost Battalion, our recon (reconnaissance) sergeant was in the foxhole not too far away from me and we caught a lot of overhead mortar fire and tree bursts. He carried the maps…of the terrain and… positions…so they called him the recon sergeant. We were laying in…our foxholes

and then I heard him screaming. Pretty soon, he pokes his head out of a foxhole and says, "Hey Kaun, I got a million dollar wound." He got some shrapnel in his butt. So off he went and next day I was the recon sergeant and somebody else was back on the radio. I was glad to shed that radio; that damn thing was heavy.

Back to civilian life – and discrimination

The 15th of June 1945, I went to Los Angeles., bought myself some city clothes and turned down a request to join the Reserves. "No," I said. "I had enough."

Back in Seattle, I wasn't too crazy about going to work at the tackle shop, especially going to work for a new entity which obviously would've been very poor pay. But there weren't other jobs that would pay worth a damn either.

Discrimination may not have been open; it was rather subtle. But I have to admit that probably Seattle was much better than what others encountered whether it was in California or whatever. Yes, the discrimination was there. There was still signs saying "No Japs wanted," that sort of thing. Make you angry as hell.

In Twin Falls, Idaho, a Caucasian friend and I worked together and we'd come in to town. And he said, "Let's go have a beer," so we went to this one tavern and sat down at the bar. This bartender said, "We won't serve you. I'll serve you, but I won't serve him" – meaning me. My friend got madder than hell. He was ready to tear up the joint and beat the bartender. In my mind, I said, if I ever come back here, I'm gonna blow this damn place up.

Interviewed by Seiji Hata and Debbie Kashino McQuilken, courtesy of Seattle Sansei.

Victorino "Victor" OVENA

Vietnam War
Army, Airborne, 8th Cavalry, 1965-1968
Specialist E-4

At first I was going to school. I didn't have enough money to go to college, so I tried to save enough money to go…All of a sudden, I had this notice: "You're being inducted to the Armed Services of the United States Army." I went to talk to the recruiter and he said, "If you enlist, then you'll have your choice of stations." I didn't want to go to Vietnam; I didn't want to go to war so I enlisted. I signed a waiver saying I was going to Germany. At that point in time, it was great. I went to Airborne training. Next thing I know, I'm on my way to Vietnam. I was 19 years old.

When you are a kid, you like to play war, and next thing you know, you're there. It's funny 'cause they told us: "You are well-trained soldiers of the United States of America. You have all this training and you're well-equipped…" We were trained like we were invincible. We were supermen. We could do anything we want. Then the first night we were there, reality set in.

Our company was being hit. We didn't know where it was coming from. You're just a rookie… You don't know anything. You don't know what it's like. It sounds like firecrackers, but firecrackers with a bigger bang. You hear people screaming because they're being hit. Men screaming – it's like a shrieking scream. It's something that haunts you once in a

We were trained like we were invincible. We were supermen. We could do anything we want. Then the first night we were there, reality set in.

while. I didn't want to be there. I wanted to be home. I closed my eyes and…I cried.

You think about happy times – just being there with your friends, going to a drive-in movie, hamburger stands, driving your car. I had a '56 Chevrolet. You think about happy memories with your family.

I came from a military family. My dad was in the Second World War and also in the Korean War. He talked about the war before but I didn't believe it. Hey, he could make it; I could make it.

My dad had a hard time talking about it, but he just told me:

"Whatever you do, don't wish there's a war. Don't ever go to war. That's the hardest thing there is." I said, well, I'm gonna be like Dad. I'm gonna be in the military. I'm gonna be a superman. I'm gonna be a hero.

The first night, we lost three people. After that, everything sets in and you say, "Okay. I'm here. I can't go home. I have a duty to perform." So your mind changes…it's kill or be killed. I'm gonna live from day to day.

But in my mind too, I was thinking: How about the other side? What are they thinking? If they're thinking about what I'm thinking, what are we doing this for? What are we trying to prove? So all these questions were going through my head. Am I trying to prove that we're better than they are, or are they just trying to survive…?

During training, it's like brainwashing. The dummy that you see is your enemy. So every time you hit that dummy you holler, "Kill Kill Kill. Them Them Them." Who's Them?

I've seen them. I've seen them face-to-face in hand-to-hand combat. I could see their eyes. They're just like me. They looked like people like me.

Why we're there, I don't know. Why he's fighting me, I don't know. But if I didn't, he would have killed me. So it's survival time. There's no time to think. There's no time at all.

My perception at the beginning of the Vietnam War was to help the people out there. In the Philippines, I'd seen poor people and how they try to survive. And then I came to the United States and all of a sudden, hey, this is a good life. This is what I have and the government's been good to me. I'm going try to protect that, to save it for the other people who are coming. Maybe spread it out to the world so it could be all like this. Then I started thinking, do the South Vietnamese people want to be like this?

The only North Vietnamese I saw was the one we captured. I saw him as a person, ordinary person. He's probably in his 40s…and he's probably thinking about his family, how he might never see them again. It's mixed emotions for me.

When we went to Vietnam…I got real close to my squad. And then it seems like you make a pact together: "We're all going home together. Whatever happens, no one's going to get left behind." In fact, we bet $20 and put it in the pot. Whoever comes back alive gets to collect that money. It's just a silly bet. You're not wishing they would die. The idea is to make sure you get back. Terry Carter, that was his name. He's the one who got killed. That really broke us apart.

On one mission, the enemy shot my friend. My rifle was gone, so I just jumped over, grabbed the gun, turned around and fired away. John Wayne style. And I got him. I didn't even look at him. When I shot him, he was like this little branch and he just fell. Left him there, didn't even look at him. Maybe he's still alive. I kept that in my head. Maybe one of his friends also dragged him out to take him home.

I got to the point where I welcomed death. You keep thinking about not making it home. Thinking about being left out there to rot, that no one would take you back. Thinking about not seeing your friends again. If I got killed, my suffering would be over. I'd be happy if I die and they bring me back home.

When I was really home, I was happy. In fact, I kissed the first girl I saw. I got slapped. Oh, it was fun. She was a WAC (Women's Army Corps). I just told her I was so happy to see somebody who wasn't going to shoot back at me. She understood.

I felt like the war was a lost cause when I came back. I felt like I went up there just for no reason at all. I thought I would have a homecoming like when they came back from World War II. You have all those pictures of this ticker tape parade. Well, it wasn't going to be that way. It's like I just wasted my time, wasted my freedom. I didn't want to talk about the war anymore. I just blocked it out of my mind and said, "Okay, as far as I can say, I didn't go there. It was just a bad nightmare, bad dream."

My kids ask me about war and I just tell them about the happy times that I had. Those are the things…that I want them to remember. There's a few times that were bad but there's always happy times. You can always isolate those things. Put the bad times away. In Vietnam, we had an open latrine. Everything is collected in this barrel and everyday, they take that out and burn the contents then put it back. When it fills up, you burn it again. The first sergeant told one of the rookies to get some gasoline from the motor pool and burn the latrine. He went up there and burned the whole thing down! Those are the things I remember that I tell my family about.

My dad and I talked when I got back from Vietnam. We shared experiences, just the two of us. I asked him, "Did this ever happen to you." Then he finally told me, yes. He said, "What you went through, I went through." So I guess history repeats itself.

Interviewed by Paula Bock.

Lorenzo Umel PIMENTEL (1909-1989)

World War II
Army, 1st Filipino Infantry Regiment, 1942-1945
Sergeant

My oldest brother came here for adventure. He asked me if I want to come to the United States for a better education. So he sent me my fare and everything I need for coming from Philippines to America. I came to America in 1928. When I was in the Philippines, I thought America was in heaven.

In 1932, the Depression started. We could hardly find a decent job. Sometimes we work part-time in a restaurant or hotel. I work in drug store, as a delivery boy, a stock boy. Work on the farm.

The Army drafted me. I liked it. When the Japanese bombed Pearl Harbor and bombed Manila, it made me mad. They formed two regiments in the West Coast. We got the 1st and 2nd Filipino Regiments. At first, I was with the American outfit. Tank destroyer was my mechanized outfit. Very soon, there was a circular that they want all Filipinos in a regiment so when I was in Texas, I transferred to the West Coast and joined the 2nd Filipino Regiment.

Preparing to save the Philippines

After three months in the 2nd Regiment, Col. Whitney, the aide of Gen. MacArthur, came into the United States from Australia and went in all those service records of Filipinos in both regiments. He found my name and put it aside and collected about 700

When the war was declared and I was in the service, I realized the advantage of being a citizen of the United States.
—*Courtesy of Pimentel Family, circa 1945.*

names of Filipinos. He called a meeting and gave us 15 minutes to decide if we want to take…a special job for that unit he selected. He told us, "Gen. MacArthur wants to see you very much." So I was inspired at the time. He said, "There is a pile of papers at the door. You pick one and read it and if you like it, sign it and if you don't like it, don't sign it." So I read it, liked it, so I signed it. After that, he called my name and then I went in front and saluted. He asked me why I signed this paper. "Because," I said, "I am a soldier. Whatever the Army wants me to do, I do it." And he said, "Good boy."

After orientation, they call me the next day, so I go to the office. Colonel told me: "You know that airplane there warming up? Go on it." He gave me two envelopes and said not to open until told to do so. When we were about the middle of the Pacific Ocean, he told us to open the envelope… My order was to go to Australia.

When we arrived at Australia…a lady and Australian girls asked what nationality I am. I told her Filipino. She didn't know about Filipino. I told her: "MacArthur boy, Gen. MacArthur boys." She asked me another question: "Did you come to die?" And I said, "No, I didn't come to die." What she meant was "today," not "to die."

She took me in a secret camp. The next morning there, a truck came to the office and…I went with the driver. He took me to downtown in Brisbane. That was where Gen. MacArthur was staying, where I met different officers. They asked me, "Do you know where you are going?" "No, sir," I said. And he told me I was going to the intelligence school. I was surprised. After all the interviews and orientation, they took me to another secret camp…and Col. Whitney was there.

We went to school there. They sent Filipinos in groups to the Philippines to work behind the enemy lines. I got a group and they sent us to the

Philippines by submarines. We went to San Fernando. They find out that many Japanese were there so we all went back north. The commander of the submarine said they were going to land us north of the mainland. It was late 1943, before the invasion of Leyte.

So we went to the bay and settled down there the whole day. Then some where around nine o'clock…we went up. Three of my crew went ashore to check the areas. When they say it was clear, we started going ashore. Before I get out of the submarine, I felt like there was ice over my back. Then when I hit the beach, I felt strong.

Reuniting with family

We keep moving all the time through mountain ranges. We keep moving all the time to get away from the Japanese. When we first reach the town…there were only two people in there, the priest and the assistant. The people move – all evacuation. So we told the priest to tell those people to get back in town because we got some news for them. People were happy to see us. We were like heroes when they saw us. They gave us flowers and everything. They gave us fruits. As soon as we reach the town, we deliver some propaganda speeches to tell the people that the Americans never forget the Filipinos. They never turned their backs. We told them, "America is working 24 hours a day. They are building ships, building big airplanes that could carry tanks and, brothers, they will be jumping from that airplane…to fight the enemy."

Then I was assigned to San Fernando. Everybody was surprised to see me. One afternoon…I went down and saw these girls and she looked like one of my cousins. They called me uncle. And then they told me that my father, my brothers, my sisters and my kid brother were members of the guerillas.

The girls didn't go home until they took me with them. I went to the evacuation area…and I saw all my relatives there. I was shaking hands with them and they opened their mouth without saying anything. I saw my sister-in-law and…I told her son: "You better go get your grandpa. Tell him to come home and don't tell him I'm here." I hid behind the back door. Instead of coming in the front door, my parents went to the back door so they caught me hiding. My own mother kept on crying. And then I asked them, "Who are my relatives that's working for the enemy?" Everybody was looking at each other and then I pointed at my father. "If you are one of them, I'm going to hang you because you are no good." That's what I told him. "I'm going to hang you right there because you are selling your country."

The regiment kept on fighting and there was a circular that all the Filipinos who have been dropped by submarines…should go to Manila to regroup. We were still fighting there and when I was in Manila, there was news that the Japanese surrendered already. The war was over.

I arrived here at Ft. Lewis Dec. 31, in the morning. The officer said those who want to go home, could go home tonight. When I got home to Seattle, I knocked on the door, nobody answered…because they were sleeping. The next morning, I went downtown, looked around. Then, some of my friends saw me. They were glad to see me in one piece. They saw me with all my decorations. They were all happy.

Before the war, Whites…don't respect Filipinos. When the war was declared and they found out those Filipinos in Bataan were fighting side by side with the Americans, that's when they respected the Filipinos. After the war, it was better for the Filipinos. They could apply for citizenship by then. First, I don't want to apply because of what I experienced…before the war. But when the war was declared and I was in the service, then I realized the advantage of being a citizen of the United States.

Interviewed by Cynthia Mejia-Guidici,
—Courtesy of Filipino American National Historical Society.

Hilarion "Don" POLINTAN

Persian Gulf War
Army, 37th Armor Battalion, 1989-1992
Specialist, E-4

In 1989, that's when I signed up with the Army. The biggest thing was the college money I could get from them and basically I was just interested. I had a few friends in the military so that's probably what pushed me towards joining. The branch that would offer me the most college funding is what I went for. I decided to go to the Army because they offered me a $30,000 college fund to spend over a 10-year period. I looked at the Navy too because travel interested me, but the college fund was not as large as what I could get from the Army.

In basic training, they still yell at you. They treat you like you're nothing, but you have to keep in mind…they don't personally think that you are scum. It's to strengthen your character. Mostly, it was just physical training where they actually get your endurance up. You had to endure some mental abuse, the yelling and all that. They would actually try to break you, to crack you as hard as they can. I knew a couple of people who were threatening to commit suicide just to get out because they can't handle the stress. But if you think about it, if you're going to war, you're going to have to handle the stress. If you can't handle the stress, the people who are with you get killed.

On the way over to Saudi Arabia, everyone felt tension, tension. We all looked at each other and realized this is real, this is what we trained for.

Everybody was like family. Everybody took care of everybody. In basic training, I was the weakest runner in my unit. And the funny thing is, I didn't complain as much. Even though I had that weakness and everyone had to wait for me, everybody respected me.

Going after Iraq's Saddam Hussein

I was kind of in denial over everyone saying that we were heading out to Saudi Arabia for war. This was November through December. I was in denial, saying, "We're not going. We're not going." Late December comes, then we get the word that we're going to be shipping out in January. All of a sudden, our jaws drop and all the wives are starting to cry, and everyone is starting to get scared. No one wanted to go to war. That's when I saw some more people doing stuff so they don't have to go. There's this one guy in my unit who actually started hitting his leg with a cane so he wouldn't go. He tried to injure himself. I think he was really scared but…we didn't have pity on him. We…ridiculed him more because he was deserting us, his team. We were taking that personally.

On the way over to Saudi Arabia, everyone felt tension, tension. We all looked at each other and realized this is real, this is what we trained for. Basically, we made a pact with each other, saying: "If anything happens, everyone's going home. Don't leave anyone behind."

We kept POW (prisoner of war) camp, where we didn't really see much resistance. Most of them weren't getting supplies, not very much food, so most of them were just giving up left and right. Most of the time, my main responsibility in my group was to make sure all tanks were going. If there was a tank broken – we know probably there would be gunfire and stuff – we had five minutes to get that tank going or burn it down.

We felt pity for the POWs because they weren't taken care of. We even had to give up voluntarily some of our own clothing to clothe the POWs. Most of them didn't have socks. Because this was done in the desert, it was either hot or freezing cold. They had torn clothes, no socks, no shoes; it was terrible. Since there was no gunfire, I felt sorry for them. I felt they were betrayed by Saddam Hussein, who we were really after.

We had missions to go out on, but only four of us had to go – like trying to look for a tank that broke down in the middle of the night. We had to be careful. Out in the desert, there are no lights anywhere. Sometimes our night-vision goggles didn't help much because it was pitch black. That was kind of scary, but luckily, no incidents happened. Being out in the desert, you don't get to take showers for days. In a way, it was an adventure for me. I took it in stride. I thought it was kind of fun.

Modern war

Missiles are very accurate nowadays. You don't need to see your enemy. I'd say it's very humane in some ways, but inhumane because you're shooting your missiles, you don't know who you're killing so it doesn't really matter. It doesn't affect you. Your humanity doesn't get affected. We were beside the laser-guided missiles. At night, all of us would be sitting outside watching the missiles like it was the 4th of July for us.

Today's kind of war will be worse, because the humanity factor will be lessened and lessened where you'll be callused. Shooting a missile here and there, you don't mind. You don't care anymore who it hits. I think it will be a bigger war. The less you see your enemy, the bigger the war will be, the more destruction there will be.

The other side of combat

There was a lighter side of the war that I don't think anyone really knew about. There was a resort that we could go to. It was something to let the guys relax and stuff. There was a swimming pool. My platoon joined the volleyball tournament, which we won. To tell you the truth, the war America saw through the TV was over-dramatized. It wasn't all that bad, I would say. TV stations were bucking for ratings. It was pretty relaxed in the war, not relaxed relaxed but the anxiety was gone. We knew our jobs. We stayed alert. It was calm pretty much. Sometimes when the sky was clear at night, by moonlight, you could actually read and write letters. It was pretty out there.

From my whole military experience, I've learned to become a stronger person, more confident in my abilities. Sometimes, a little arrogant. All in all, I think my experience in the Army was a benefit to myself, and my family. I owe a lot to the Army.

Interviewed by Pei Pei Sung and Geneva Witzleben.

Robert Satoshi SATO

World War II
Army, 100th Battalion, 442nd Regimental Combat Team, 1944-1946
Staff Sergeant

Our boyhood days were pretty tough. We all worked on the farm. Everybody worked hard like that, and it was a relatively happy period. At the same time, I think we were always aware of the greater White community's attitudes about Japanese…even before Pearl Harbor.

On Dec. 7, 1941, our whole family was out in the field working, and then we came home, had dinner. With my older sister and brother, I went to a movie. During the showing of the movie, they stopped the film and said, "All servicemen, report to base." It was only after we came out that we found out the bombing had occurred.

We know we're Americans, but we also have close feelings for Japan because after all, that's where our parents came from. We were caught in the middle. You want to be proud of your heritage. Yet, when the barrage of things that were said tries to make you feel less than a full being, then it doesn't make you feel very good. So I think we as Niseis [second generation Japanese Americans] – at least I felt this way – we were always kind of on guard. We kept saying to ourselves, "We're Americans," but we knew we were not being perceived as such by the general public. There

During evacuation, I remember Dad saying, 'I don't know what's going to happen to us, but remember: This is your country and you have to act accordingly.'

was this constant barrage of hysterical reporting [about rumored acts of sabotage]. We were made to feel we were the enemy.

During evacuation of Japanese Americans from the West Coast, I remember my dad saying, "I don't know what's going to happen to us, but remember: This is your country and you have to act accordingly." It was tough for him to say it because he didn't talk about those kinds of things to us. So we went on to concentration camp. In Camp Harmony [Puyallup, Wash.], we were outside the main fairground and our camp was surrounded by these high barbed wire fences with watchtowers and machine guns at each of the four corners.

My feeling about evacuation and internment was one of utter disappointment in the country and in the people because we grew up with quite a few lessons on what democracy was. We were taught the melting pot theory and all that. But when the war broke out, everything changed for us. So then it became a matter of, if you weren't a White American, somehow civil rights and other Constitutional privileges didn't apply to you. It was really a time to question what kind of a country we lived in.

I finished my senior high school in the Minidoka Concentration Camp. We had graduation about July of 1943. I think July '43 was a few months after people like my older brother had volunteered and left for the 442nd Regimental Combat Team. I didn't volunteer then. I wanted to finish high school. I went out and worked on the farm for a few months because I figured it was just a question of time before I'd get drafted. I was 19.

In the Army

I remember we were on the train going to Camp Shelby, Miss., on D-Day, June 6, 1944. We had probably one of the shortest training session of any group. I had nine weeks of basic training. End of August, we were told, "Hey, you guys are going to go overseas. We'll give you one week furlough." I went home to camp. I was in uniform and I had to have a GI sentry pass me through the gate at Minidoka. My mother was there. My dad had gone to work outside the camp, working for a turkey farmer in a little place called Gooding, Idaho. I went out to visit my dad, slept in his trailer, which was out there in the middle of the sage brush because he was a shepherd to 4,000 turkeys. I didn't tell Mom or Dad I was going overseas, although my dad did write to me after I was overseas – the one and only letter he ever wrote to me. He said something about how he appreciated the fact that I had visited him. He suspected I was going overseas. I guess he just told me to take care of myself.

Suffering in the war zone

When I first got to France in October 1944, we entered through LeHarve harbor. From the bombed out pier area, we had to walk at night. We walked holding the guy in front because it was so dark. This was now getting into the war zone. We ended up in what used to be a cabbage field. We stayed there three, four days until the regiment sent trucks after us. But during that time, it was really a shock. We were living in these tents and all we had to do was sit there and eat. Then, when you got done, you went to the garbage can to dump out the leftovers. When you went to the garbage cans – this is the first time I experienced this – the French people were there with their pans, and they were just begging for any leftover so they could take it home and feed their family.

The French and Italian hills, they're terraced, like steps. The natives had built up these rock walls to form the rise and they would farm on the little steps. So on the last push to Italy in April 1945, we're going up the mountainside in the dark. The guy in the lead probably has some kind of…flashlight or a local guide and the rest of us are hanging on to the pack of the guy in front. Next morning at five minutes to five – that was our jump-off time, that's when we attack. At five minutes to five, they said, the artillery was going to open up.

So we're sitting up there waiting, and five minutes to five comes around. Gee, we had rockets, artillery and what they call long toms, the long-range artillery. And they're back there…maybe 10 miles behind us but everything opened up at one time. It's pitch black, and next minute, the sky is filled with all these shells going, the flashing of the guns going off, the bursting of the shells beyond us. And it was just like from pitch-black night to broad daylight. It was that bright. Then they let up and we started running forward. Then, the Germans opened up on us.

I had a couple of shells come in real close, but I heard them coming so I was able to duck. It got my lieutenant. He got hit in the chest and he came rolling into this hole that my squad was in. He said, "Shoot me, shoot me." He was in such pain and I don't know if he survived or not.

Returning to the U.S.

After the war, that's one of my disappointments. My parents were still in a farm labor camp in Twin Falls, Idaho. I've talked to different groups about my experiences and I said, "You know, most of the time when you're in the service of a victorious army, you come home to your home. But here I am, coming home to a farm labor camp, way out there in Idaho." So our home wasn't home. Home was where the parents were, but that's about all I can say.

Interviewed by Pei Pei Sung.

Martin J. SIBONGA, SR.

World War II
Army, Parachute Infantry Regiment, 1943-1946
Private 1st Class

I was a 1930s Chinatown orphan. I had excema and rickets so bad that I couldn't go to school. Eventually, child welfare services sent me to the old orthopedic hospital and the Seattle Children's Home. My last juvenile residency was at the Briscoe School for Boys near Kent, Wash.

By 1943, I volunteered for quick induction. High school hadn't been much fun anyway. Elementary school had been interrupted so often by excema and then asthma that I was draft age as a freshman. I was drafted in February. I didn't want any desk job in the military. I wanted to get in there and be like John Wayne, and do all the heroic things that the movies pushed on. So when the call came out for volunteers for paratroops, I made the big move with a half dozen other guys. The rest razzed us by calling us "suicide troops" and "cannon fodder." But it was the only option away from menial warehouse and KP jobs.

Jump school was a rigorous process of testing you all the way, keeping you on the threshold of pain and still asking you to run farther, do a few more push-ups. Go, go, go all the time. And I think what drove me was…never being able to do anything – too damn small for the high school football teams. At that time, the paratroopers were all six-footers and quite athletic, so it was nice

I remember the guys who were there and the good times when we drank together, ate together, woke up frozen on the ground together.

to find out that, by God, I could keep up with them and keep on going when others would drop out. That was the biggest accomplishment that I enjoyed. Oh, hell, I was scared sure. But scared worse of the shame of failure and the scorn and the ridicule I'd be subject to for chickening out.

My first introduction to the Army Airborne was being rejected outright by the 511th Parachute Infantry Regiment, which was processing its way through Camp Toccoa. I had the last laugh on them when they ended up in the Pacific, fighting "little guys" like me! As rejects, we spent time with the "out platoon," along with the malcontents, the lazy, inept or drunk. We had all the crummiest details and were treated like we shouldn't have been around there.

A chance at paratrooper

A call came for someone who could paint a sign. A new colonel had arrived to form a new regiment to replace the departing 511th. I'd done a little bit of drawing, so I tried that, painted the colonel's sign. He asked what the hell was I doing there – probably didn't say it in those words, but he started talking to me. It was my chance to tell him my sad tale and he gave me a chance to try for paratroop rank, despite my 120-pound, 5'4" stature and sixth grade education. Making it through jump school at Fort Benning was an unforgettable achievement of my life. And the $50 extra jump pay wasn't bad either.

In a way, going into combat was like going into a Fourth of July circus. We marched up at night. The closer we got, the booms of artillery got louder. Conversation would go up and down the column. "Hey, listen to that. That's a damn big one." The closer we got, we could hear machine guns and there was a definite difference between quick-firing German MD-34s and our old sputtering .30 calibers.

It was a night approach and we had to reach a mountain where we dug in. Luckily, the Germans were in continuous retreat, so we didn't have any major engagements. In the Italian countryside, even lowly farmhouses had their roofs blown off and holes in stone walls. Still, the birds flew around and sung.

We were an orphan outfit. We had some independent missions, but usually we'd be attached to wherever needed. We were in the supplemental role primarily of the big operations leading into Germany. Our big jump on Aug. 15, 1944, into southern France has been touted as the most successful airborne operation. There were so many of us scattered far and wide that this dispersion worked against German defenses. We attacked from all over the country, disrupting or destroying the enemy from unexpected locations.

Unfortunately, there was fog and no contact with the pathfinder jumpers who usually land before us to set up beacons. Some troopers stayed in the air for an hour before they hit the ground. In my case, I had barely enough time to see my canopy open before I hit the rock wall of a French vineyard. I sprained my ankle and was in agony. I joined the other wounded until we were gathered the next morning and shipped down to Naples into an Army hospital for a lousy sprained ankle. I was in a group with about seven. We all went to different homes. They took care as best as they could have a sprained ankle, and put me in a feather bed. I got a great night's sleep, serenaded by the family's two charming daughters singing French songs. The people were just great to us.

Then, we were sent to the Alpes Maratames, the mountains on the border between France and Italy. We had to pack water, rations and ammunition on hills that goats couldn't climb! We were relieved by the 442nd Regimental Combat Team and sent north to get ready for what turned out to be the big one: the Battle of the Bulge. But I caught the flu and stayed behind. The Luftwaffe bombed and strafed our warehouse. It was really a front-row seat to a show of horizon-to-horizon four-engine bombers heading for Germany. The whole sky was just drumming from the engines – very spectacular. It was bumper to bumper with traffic moving north, tanks, tanks, tanks and artillery – all of the abundance of the American arsenal.

Bonds that last

Now, 50 years later, I remember the guys who were there and the good times when we drank together, ate together, woke up frozen on the ground together, and tried to get warm or get dry, shared a dugout together. And with that, you have a respect and belonging and an appreciation for one another that just lasts. You appreciate it. It's like being on a football team, basketball team. You play and sported hell together and pull out of adversity, and you have a comradeship that lasts the rest of your life.

Interviewed by Ken Mochizuki.

–Courtesy of Martin J. Sibonga, Sr., 1946.

Lorenzo "Larry" W. SILVESTRE

Vietnam War, Persian Gulf War
Marine Corps, 2nd Battalion Night Marines, 1967-1990
Master Sergeant

My whole family is in the Coast Guard, except my dad; he's in the Army. And no offense to the Army, but I don't like the Army that much. I like the Marine Corps uniform. Plus, I don't like water so I didn't join the Coast Guard or Navy. I went into the service March 3rd, 1967. I graduated that summer in boot camp and went to advance training in Camp Pendleton, Calif. From there, I went straight to Vietnam.

Out of the whole company of Marines training in boot camp, I was the only Oriental. I was scared. Really, I was scared 'cause all these guys – the Blacks, Whites, Samoans – and I'm the shortest one. I really don't want to think about it because there was a lot of prejudice when I was in boot camp. I was called names. I was called gook. I was called monkey. I was called everything in the book. I was singled out because I was Oriental. The drill instructor told me: "You will not last in the Marine Corps." I said, "Well try me." And I did try. I went through hell with those instructors. The dirtiest job they got in the platoon, I got 'em. Peel potatoes and all that crap. I was here peeling potatoes by myself, the rest of the guys would go somewhere. At night time, I was just lying there, thinking about it, just saying, "I hope

the next day it will be better"...until I graduated. When I graduated boot camp, I told that drill instructor I would be coming back. He told me: "You'll die over there." I said, "I'll look for you when I come back. I got a grudge and I'm going to settle that grudge when I come back."

The first day back from Vietnam, I went back and tried to see him but he wasn't there. He had motivated me to come back – not to kill him or anything like that. I wanted to go back and really, I wanted to thank him for what he did to me to keep me alive.

Going in country

I was there in November '67. Landed in Da Nang. Within a week I was a veteran. I was in a firefight within a week. In fact, my whole company was almost annihilated at that time. The first time I was in there, we got about 25 people left in my company still walking...out of close to 200 people. We just walked into a trap. It's bodies all over. And that's the first time I ever killed anybody out there. It was pretty close. I thought I was in a movie, like a John Wayne movie. It was not real. People screaming and dropping off like flies, blood all over. It really was pretty rough for me that first week 'cause I don't know what the hell I'm doing out there anyway. I was really shaken by that. No introduction. Just right there. Just went to the war and started fighting.

I thought I was in a movie, like a John Wayne movie. It was not real.

We went through training but I didn't see it that way, that war was just like a big mess, with everybody yelling. In training, they say, "The enemy's on the left, shoot on the left, shoot on the right." In real combat, I don't even know what I'm supposed to do, so I just keep shooting right in front of me.

I was with the Night Marines 13 months and out of that 13 months, the only time I left the combat zone was when I went to the Philippines for five days R & R.

When I got my first kill, I threw up. I was scared. This is how the people died? And after about two or three kills, it flows. It's just like nothing. It's just a body. When I was on patrol, sometimes I would be by myself. They say I look like Vietnamese so the Vietnamese won't bother me. I carry a .45 and a knife. That's one of the things I really don't want to think about because when I go out there, I intend to kill somebody. Either they kill me or I kill them. I would crawl and try to follow them. I wait and wait and wait until they fall asleep and then I crawl in. I'd say I cut their throat too many times. I don't see their faces. All I could feel is blood coming out of my hand. When I cut him, I held his face and cut him and the blood wouldn't stop flowing. It's kind of warm, warm blood.

I was a tunnel rat. My size is good for tunnel rat because I'm small and thin. I come down the tunnel and check it out. I go in there to eliminate whatever they got inside the tunnel. I shoot whatever moves or I stab them. That's what my job is. As soon as I finish, I put charges on that tunnel…and then blow it. A lot of times, you can walk in the big tunnels. Sometimes, just barely, I could squeeze myself in the tunnel. Going inside, I would think that I might not be able to come out again because it's so tight. But as soon as you pass… five to 10 feet, those squeeze type, you come into a big tunnel.

'I was the only one without a scratch.'

I made friends and it's my mistake to make friends over there. They get killed. Once, when we were in a foxhole, we got hit. We were playing cards and rounds hit us directly where we were playing. One of the guys just had a baby. He got a telegram a few days earlier: "Congratulations you have a son." He lost both of his arms that day.

I got thrown out of the foxhole and every time I stuck my head out, it was rounds and everything all over the place. I heard screaming. I was crying because I couldn't do anything. I went in there and I was still crying. I saw a foot sticking out of the rubble and I thought somebody was underneath. I started digging in, my hand bleeding and everything else. I pulled that leg, certain that somebody's attached to that leg. All I got was a piece of leg. I was shaking. I was in shock. I was holding the leg of a buddy of mine and he was down below the hill. I went down and picked him up and this thing won't leave my mind.

I was the only one without any scratch. And I feel guilty about that. I really do. That's why I was going to this therapy. Knowing that those people…either got killed or wounded and I'm still alive. I was there 15 months, never got a scratch. I always volunteered to go out by myself but nothing happened to me.

When I enlisted in the Marine Corps, I thought it was just like a John Wayne picture, but it was a hell different from the movies. World War II and those movies that you see, you don't see nothing in there like people getting sick because of the war; they come back and they're just normal. Killing people is – I don't know how to explain it. I killed too many people out there. That's what's bothering me. I was sent over there to do a job and I was doing it but it's still bothering me right now.

Interviewed by Jose Velasquez and Pei Pei Sung.

–Courtesy of Lorenzo Silvestre, 1968.

Pete SUA

Vietnam War
Marine Corps, 3rd Battalion Night Marines, 1966-1970
Corporal

I was in San Francisco visiting with my cousin and we were discussing the war and what we felt about the people of South Vietnam. I was sitting there watching TV one day and then President Kennedy made his speech: "Ask not what your country can do for you, ask what you can do for your country." When John Kennedy made that speech, I really felt an obligation to the country. I had a lot of uncles in the Army, my dad was in the Air Force, and I had some uncles in the Navy, and I always heard the Marine Corps was the fastest way to get to Vietnam. I guess I wanted to see action and I wanted to do something worthwhile. I wasn't gung-ho to go over there and die, but I wanted to go over there and see what I could do for the people.

During training, they do a lot of mental training. They yell; you jump. They give you an order; you jump. They showed us a lot of movies, what the war was all about and about "Charlie." Charlie was always the bad guy. But when you grow up in Samoa, you have your own way of thinking. All through my training, I took the physical part to heart, but the message I was focused on was this is for my country. The people down south don't want the people up north to come down and tell them what to do, so we're there to help those people out.

My dad called up the VA office and said, 'This ain't my son.' Before, I was always happy-go-lucky. The war took my humor away.

'I thought I was in hell.'

I did my 13-month tour, but I got interrupted in the middle of my tour. We took some incoming and my bunker was standing in the line of fire. I got hit right with the ammo, which was right next to my bunker, and I went up with it and woke up in Japan. I have flashes of my body just being on fire, my face on fire, my hands on fire, and I'm rolling. I'm in the gurney on the outside of the chopper, flying through the air. I didn't know I was later put on the airplane. All I saw were I.V. bottles and gurneys. I thought we were going to hell someplace, 'cause all I heard was screaming. I thought I was in hell. And then I woke up in Japan. It was a trip because when I came to and saw a nurse with one of those caps on her head, I said, "Oh, thank you, God. I'm in heaven." And they all kind of looked at me and go, "No, you're in Yokosuka, Japan."

They treated all my burns. It was an experience, a shock. After lying in bed for two, three weeks, finally getting out, and going to look at yourself in the mirror. Freddy Krueger [from the movie, "Nightmare on Elm Street"] – that's what I saw. I saw my face all discolored, disfigured. I never thought I was going to have my face back. I went into a deep depression and they were telling me, "Oh no, we'll fix you." I looked like a mummy. They would wrap up my whole body, my face, my hands. The only bad scar I got is right around my back where I guess the powder charge landed.

At the hospital, I was told I was going home, and then I got back on the airplane and it was headed back to 'Nam.

A different man

At first, when I got in country, I was throwing candies to the kids coming towards us in the villages and I was taking pictures. When we got ambushed on the way out, I had a camera in my hand and not my M-14. But the second time I went, I had my weapon ready. The second time around, I didn't even blink an eye. It was just two different people. The guy that came the first time was sort of adventurous; the guy that came back the second time was serious about his mission. After seeing so many people die, you get kind of cold. In order to stay alive, I learned to fear and fear was what kept me going.

In my heart, I wanted to be close to my squad, but I had trained myself to be ice-cold with anybody. After a while, it wasn't your mission to conquer anybody. My mission was just to kill the enemy, get these guys home alive, and get myself home alive. When I came back from the hospital, I was more in tune with what the war was really about. I just didn't want to feel close to anybody anymore, after my corpsman, Todd Richards, got his head blown off.

I met Todd after I'd been there about eight months. He went out with me on most of my patrols. I guess we got close. We had plans of making some music, going to Hawaii and just running on the beach and surfing, and going back to Samoa and living in a shack. The way he got killed – it just took a lot out of me. It was supposed to be my last patrol. We were both getting ready to rotate out of the front line. Usually, you have a point man and your first fight team, then me, then my radio man, then my corpsman. I walked point, he walked where I was supposed to be at. Since he was walking in the squad leader position, when we got opened up on…he caught a round and it just took his head off. I turned around, all I saw was his brains splattered and the skin from the back of his head hanging over his backpack. I blacked out. Just to turn around and see his head explode – it kind of kills something in you.

Haunted by war

When I did come home, my parents didn't recognize me. My dad called up the VA (Veterans Affairs) office and said, "This ain't my son." Before, I was always happy-go-lucky. The war took my humor away. I had trouble back here in the States. I wanted to go back to Vietnam. I was getting in trouble. I left on a weekend pass and I just stayed away about a week and they picked me up and said, "You're AWOL" (absent without leave). I just had a lot of things on my mind. I was feeling alienated. I wasn't used to the world anymore. Every time I went into a bar, I got into fights.

I didn't find out until 1978 that I had post-traumatic stress disorder. After I finished processing with myself and my friends, then I started processing with the other side. The North Vietnamese and Vietcong had families. They were fighting for what they thought was right, and I was fighting on this side for what I thought was right. Some of those people over there are doing the same thing, missing their sons or missing their fathers who got killed. You feel guilty 'cause your friends got killed and you didn't get killed, and then you turn around and you start feeling guilty because you killed somebody's father or somebody's son.

At first, I had a lot of regrets, but through all the counseling programs and going through all the things that I've learned after I got help and stuff – no, I have no regrets. Life goes on, you learn as you go, take things as they come, and then you try to make it better. I've learned a lot and I've got a lot in me that I can pass on to my fellow Samoans and my kids. They ask me about the war a lot, and I try to explain to them what they can understand, what it was all about. As they grow, they'll learn and I can be there to explain.

Interviewed by Michael Park, Carina A. del Rosario and Melissa Lin.

Shokichi "Shox" TOKITA

Vietnam War
Air Force, 1954-1978
Colonel

One of the significant things I remember about the Japanese American concentration camp was all the gold-star mothers, their flags with the stars on them [representing sons who were killed in World War II]. I remember Ben Kuroki coming in a parade through the camp one time. I think he was B-17 tail gunner. There was a lot of frowning as well as cheering because he was in the Pacific Theater, so he was fighting against Japan. There was a lot of resentment from the older folks.

When we were in camp, there were a lot of movies about war. Newspapers and comics were full of war and so a lot of our games had to do with war. We had toy guns and then we'd use sling shots, too, to play war. I don't remember too much about who was who, but I know I played the bad part as well – or the enemy, I should say.

As we were growing up later in the International District [in Seattle, Wash.], the Korean conflict was starting to take place. A lot of the guys right ahead of us in school were being drafted...on a regular basis, so the military service was pretty much uppermost in my mind – everybody's mind my age.

I didn't want to pack a rifle – that's primarily why I wound up in the Air Force. Actually, when you really get down to it, I was a draft dodger. I went to the University of Washington for two years but I didn't do very well.

I didn't want to go to Vietnam, but I knew everybody had to have a tour. So I accepted it as part of my job.

In December of '53, when I finished that fall quarter, I got a notice from the draft board. In those days, you had a deferment, a student deferment of 1S. And then I got the notice that I had been reclassified as 1A. That means I was eligible for the draft. I said, well, I don't want to go into the Army, so I was wondering what to do. I didn't want to go into the Air Force for four years – that was too long. At that time, a guy name Jim Hino had just gone through flight school in the Air Force. He was home on leave at the time and we started talking. He said, "When you qualify and get through flight school, you get your wings and you get your commission. You still have to serve for four years, but you are on flying status. And there are a lot more advantages in that." I looked into it and I wasn't sure if I wanted to stay for four years, but I'll go see if I qualify. I passed everything: written test, physicals and everything. So then I got notice that I could go into the Air Force to go through flight school. That's how it all started.

By the time I got on the plane headed on down to San Antonio [Texas] to Lackland to basic training, I found out that if you did not get through flight school...then you would just serve out the balance of two years and be discharged. I thought I'd just get into flight school and then I'd just get out; I wouldn't complete flight school. But by the time you get through flight school, you make a whole lot of friends... and it's pretty competitive. Those who actually can't make it get washed out and then pride takes over and you don't want to get washed out. By that time, I wanted to finish school. By that time also, we were flying and I really enjoyed flying. My whole attitude changed about serving four years. Flying was something I enjoyed and I got paid for.

Missile duty

We were missile combat crew. We were monitoring the ICBMs, Inter Continental Ballistic Missiles. We didn't know where it was targeted for, but they had a range of 5,000 to 8,000 miles, so we were assuming that they were aimed at Russia. We were trained to launch those and maintain the alert for the U.S. Air Force. I didn't think too much [about the destructive capability of the bomb we carried]. I mean, it was my job. It was either that or we get bombed. I'd rather strike first and be in the position to do the striking. I know the destructive force was much, much more than Hiroshima or Nagasaki – way more. And the capabilities of hitting a lot of different targets was all there. Did I have any qualms? No, I don't think so; it was either them or us.

I was given a short leave of absence to finish school because the missile program was designed so that all those officers who didn't have degrees could, on their days off, go through school to get their degrees. I got my engineering degree. I was just short of one semester or something so they allowed me to go ahead and finish school, then I went to Vietnam in 1970.

Flying in country

I didn't want to go there, but I knew...everybody had to have a tour. I accepted it as part of my job. Was I scared? No. I knew I had to go. I didn't have any special feelings about it at all. It was just part of my job.

The missions that scared me were the ones when we were flying into remote bases in country. In a lot of the remote bases that we had to fly supply mission into, those were the ones that were scary, mostly because the air field was not a regular air field. Some were paved, but most were not and they were short.

–Courtesy of Shokichi Tokita, 1955.

A couple times, we landed and the Vietcong knew we were there so they started launching incoming artillery, but we were always able to turn around and get everything unloaded. A couple times, we had to unload while we were taking off because it was just getting too close. The plane was designed so that you could put your ramp down and all the supplies would just roll on out as we barreled down the runway. We could hear the shelling bumping, getting closer. One time, I just saw some dirt flying over on the side and that was pretty close, I thought, but it was nothing like the Army guys in the trenches. The only thing I was afraid of was if I was ever shot down. Of course, as a joke, I always used to say that my survival gear was black pajamas, which was the uniform of the Vietcong.

I think the most destructive was the B-52s with their bombs. I couldn't believe what the countryside looked like after they got through. You could see it; it was just like the moon. Just no vegetation at all and it was just huge pock marks where the bombs exploded in the ground. I can't believe anybody could live through that thing.

Protecting a way of life

Our rationale was that that's why we were there, so people in our country… can demonstrate and protest what the politicians are having us do. We're in Vietnam to keep the war away from our country so that the American people can continue to do the things they want to do. This is our job: to make sure that the war didn't get closer to the U.S. It's to protect our way of life, basically.

When I talked about my career in the Air Force, I had a variety of things that I did do. It wasn't all just being a soldier. I did a lot of different things: flew in jets; flew in transports; flew in combat; worked in missiles; and worked as an engineer and comptroller. Did I have a good time? Yes! I had a real good time.

Interviewed by Ken Mochizuki and Heather Goheen.

Jimmie A. TOY

World War II
Air Force, 14th Air Service Group (a.k.a. "Flying Tigers"), 1942-1945
Sergeant

My father served in the First World War with the 94th division. He served in France as a cook. He told me when I went to enlist that I should sign on as a mess cook or supply sergeant. You don't have to worry about eating as a cook and you don't have to worry about the supply if you are a supply sergeant. But stay out of the infantry – that's hell.

[After completing overseas training and different Air Force technical schools], I was told to put on gear and march off. We went down a train and down to the boat. That was where I saw a whole bunch of Chinese Americans on board ship. I figured out we might go to China or somewhere in the Pacific. Our ship stopped in Cape Town, South Africa, for a couple of days. On the ship, the food was lousy – typical British foods. It was not a pleasant trip and it was a rough ride for 30 days. It shouldn't take that long. They were zigzagging to avoid the submarines. We didn't know where we were going. They just kept us in the dark. We then made various stops, one in Bombay, India, on February of 1944. Then we traveled across India to Calcutta by train. We finally flew over the "hump" and landed in Kunming, China.

My first assignment in China was to go to Wuchow, Kwangsi, with another

One day, they just told us to put on our gear and we marched off. We went down to a train... and then down to a boat. That was where I saw a whole bunch of Chinese Americans.

soldier to set up a lookout and warning post to report enemy airplanes seen leaving White Cloud Airport in Canton. We had an old building that they let us use. At the bottom, we set up a little station. One day, the Japanese...started dropping bombs. We had a cave where we stored our gasoline, so we went in there. It was dumb. I mean, if they hit the side of the mountain, then the gasoline would have exploded. We stayed hidden inside the cave. They got so close that we had a mosquito net on our window...blew off. It was the first time I was in a fire. It seemed like a few minutes. They came down and made a couple of passes and they were gone. Of course, we...had a machine gun but it was no good. It was like throwing rocks at them. Now after that, the Japanese broke through. They came up and took a number of places. Pretty soon after that, we had to evacuate. We went back up to Tenchuo and pulled out.

It was pretty good sometimes to be a Chinese American in China because we had the option of either wearing a uniform or civilian clothing. I chose to take the route of not wearing a uniform. I usually just wore khakis and tried to blend in. In a way, I had a better chance of avoiding capture.

Commanders signed me up on a mission...because I am Chinese and I can speak Chinese. I didn't have any opportunity to turn it down...or volunteer.

Fellow soldiers always like me when we were going to the town. I can speak and take them to places. I know where to go to eat good food...so they usually hang around with me.

When I was in Tanchuck, Kwangsi, a captain with the Chinese Air Force was directed to take me and another soldier to Wuchow. He was assigned to escort us and make arrangements for our housing and transportation. On our way down, I found out that the captain was from Toisan and he spoke to me in Toisanese, a local Chinese dialect which I happened to speak. He asked me if I was married and I said no. Then he asked, "How would you like to meet my sister?" I met his sister and we hit it off. Later, we became engaged but I had to call the engagement off because when I told my captain that I was engaged to a local girl, he told me that it was a touchy situation. He warned me, telling me that because of my duties, she could be a spy and I would then be sent to another location to serve. I was able to continue my service in Wuchow but had to leave the area because of the advancing Japanese forces. It was over two-and-a-half years before we saw each other again. We were married in San Francisco on Jan. 25, 1947.

On Armistice Day, Aug. 17, 1945, the Chinese put on shows for us. They welcomed us to a village where there was an honor guard. And they all treated us to a big banquet to show their appreciation.

I was discharged Nov. 10, 1945, and I returned to Seattle. While I was overseas, I contracted malaria and I was considered a disabled veteran. I used the GI bill and went to University of Washington for four years. At that point, I went to work for the government. I retired after 29 years of service with the U.S. Department of Housing and Urban Development.

I have two children now. I had one pass away. Vincent Chin Toy. He was in the Vietnam War. His number came up and he was drafted. It didn't occur to me that the war was unpopular when he went. It was in 1968 or '69. He was in for about three years. He was presented with an Air Force commendation medal by distinguishing himself as a ground radio operator for the 22nd Tactical Air Support Squadron. He didn't talk much about the situation over there. He was always quiet anyway. He passed away at the VA (Veterans Affairs) hospital shortly he after he got out.

Interviewed by Ron Chew and Mei Mei Kam.

Jimmy A. Toy featured with his new wife, Barbara Wong, in San Francisco Examiner, *1947. –Courtesy of Jimmie A. Toy.*

Fe TRIAS

Persian Gulf War
Navy Reserves, Navy Cargo Handling Battalion 5, 1975-1999
Hospital Corpsman 1st Class

When we were in high school in the Philippines, they would ask what we want to do. I said I want to be an accountant. I had no idea that I'm going to join the Navy. I was living with my brother at that time and he's was going to be stationed in Okinawa and I don't have anywhere to go. My other brother that came with me, he was joining the Navy also, so I decided to might as well join. I had a heck of a time because it was scary. You can talk in English, but you know how Asian people are; we have an accent. I'm afraid that I might get lost, but I made it.

Training with mostly Caucasians

I came here in May of 1975. I joined the Navy in November of 1975 and then went to boot camp. Sometimes I cried because when I went there, it was my first Christmas in the United States. I'm in boot camp. People have their families, but I don't have. So all I do is I sit there and cry, "What did I do to myself?"

Sometimes drill instructors tell you, "Do it, do it, do it." They won't give you no break. But what can you do? You're in training so you just have to go along. When I joined, the leaders are usually White people. Most of my co-sailors are White. The commanders give me all the tasks, the hardest tasks. While the White people are just emptying the garbage, I have to scrub the tub, the showers, scrub the floor and the barracks. But for them, they have to just wipe the table. They're given easy jobs and I'm here working hard. That started from the beginning and never changed. That's why I say, "Hey there's something going on." But at that time, I didn't say anything to anybody. You know how it is back then; they might give you more work.

When you go to the Philippines, they know that you're Navy, you're a big shot. But they don't know that it is really hard.

In 1975, I wasn't a swimmer. I float. When they give you a swim test, if you don't pass, they'll send you back. So what I do, right after my academic class, I go and try to swim every afternoon, every afternoon until I know how to do it. Like I said, I never swim back home, but I float. They passed me after I did it six times.

Father is a forgotten hero

My dad fought in the Vietnam War for the U.S. and they don't help him out. I even wrote a letter to…everybody in the whole Senate and they didn't do a damn thing. I felt so sorry for him because he fought in the Vietnam War. He risked his life. When he went to the Philippines, they ask him how come he can't get his citizenship. The U.S. government says…the Philippines didn't forward the proper papers to the United States. And the Philippines are saying that everything has been forwarded to the United States. My dad has the paper work and everything. And he stayed here at least eight to nine years just to fight for it but it didn't go nowhere.

Thinking of risks, hoping for peace

I haven't been in a combat situation. It's scary but this is my job. I don't have any choice. I signed my papers saying I'll do anything to help and that's all I need to do.

I don't want to watch war movies. Sometimes I watch to see what's going on about Saddam Hussein [president of Iraq which the U.S. fought in the Persian Gulf War]. It's just too stressful thinking about it. I have kids. I have a husband. What's going to happen if I…go there and something happens to me. But it is really an experience for me that I joined the Navy. It's really a good experience and I like what I'm doing. I've been meeting people and I like to travel and things like that. When you go to the Philippines, they know that you're Navy, you're a big shot. But they don't know that it is really hard.

Interviewed by Pei Pei Sung.

Stan TSUJIKAWA

Korean War
Army, 8055 Mobile Army Surgery Hospital, 1950-1952
Corporal

I can still remember that Sunday, Dec. 7, 1941. I was washing our family car, listening to the radio. That was when they announced the bombing of Pearl Harbor. I couldn't believe it. That evening...the FBI came and picked up my dad. Some things stick to your mind and I can remember listening to the radio and...Esther Litta was playing and there was a knock on the door. There were two men who came and handcuffed my dad. He was a veteran of the Russo-Japanese War. He was quite active over here at church and the Japanese Association and even Vegetable Grower's Association. Later, he was released from an internment camp in Missoula, Mont., and joined the family at the Tule Lake internment camp.

Volunteering to be shipped out

After internment at Tule Lake and Camp Minidoka, I was drafted into service in 1951 during the Korean conflict. I was expecting it. I didn't try to avoid it or anything like that. It never occurred to me that I should do that. I took basic training

You could tell when we would start getting casualties in because during the night, you could see the top of hillside light up and you could hear...fighting going on.

at Camp Atterbury, Ind., then trained in heavy mortars. After training, the war in Korea was going pretty strong. We had orders to ship out. My orders were suddenly cancelled and I was reassigned to the base hospital.

I really had a pretty easy job after I got up to the hospital because I was a ward master of this asthma and dermatologist ward. I could have stayed there all my enlistment because all we had to do was be there in the morning, assign the jobs, then sit and drink coffee with the doctors. Then after a while – I don't know why – there were rumors going around that people were going to be sent to Korea. I said, "Don't threaten me; I'll volunteer." Confident that I would be stationed in Japan, being a Nisei [second generation Japanese American], I volunteered for the Far East. I lasted three days in Japan and I was sent right over there to Korea.

Naturally, we went by ship and we landed in Inchon, which does not have a harbor so we had to wait 'til the tide was right. We went ashore on a barge. I must admit I was kind of scared, not knowing what to expect. The commanding officer got us into a little room and they asked us what we wanted to be...I just told him I wanted to cook. I didn't know anything about it. They did put me into cooking for a while and it was nice. But at that time, the war was going on. Those who had been there for a while were rotated home. And they were getting short of men and they saw my...medical experience so they put me into the hospital and I was assigned to the 8055 Mobile Army Surgical Hospital (MASH), located just below the 38th parallel. Of course, that was another experience.

You could tell when we would start getting casualties in because during the night, you could see the top of hillside light up and you could hear...fighting going on. Just when the sun starts to come up, you could hear these choppers bringing the wounded in and then they come in an ambulance. You see some pretty bad injuries. Naturally, most of us are not used to seeing open wounds and the dead and amputees. I was the type who…probably would have fainted. And in order to be able to get used to it…I used to go into the surgery and just watch them do everything until I got sick. Then, I'd run outside until everything felt better and then I'd go right back in there. I kept doing that until I got to the point where I could stand seeing all that blood and amputations. It's not that pretty. You get to the point where – I think it's kind of bad – you get kind of callous. When a soldier died, you tell the corpsman to take him to the morgue without any emotions, but deep inside, you felt sorry for the family when they received the Killed-in-Action notice. Seemed like callousness sometimes but that's what war is.

Our shift at the hospital was a 12-hour shift: nine to nine. And after you get through, you're in your tent. That was the time when you'd start thinking a little bit about home. Generally, when you're doing your job, you didn't have too much time to think about that. What I used to think of was…what my friends were doing.

My experience in the Korean War made me a better person and made me appreciate life. After you see these soldiers die…all I know is war is hell. Especially when you see the young kids get blown up to pieces, lose their arm, lose their leg. You know they have to live the rest of their life like that. I just hope I made it a little more comfortable for them.

Interviewed by Pei Pei Sung.

—Courtesy of Stan Tsujikawa, 1951.

Jose VELASQUEZ

Vietnam War
Army, 82nd Airborne, 1966-1969
Sergeant E-5

I wanted to go to school, back to college. With my father being an NCO, non-commissioned officer, there's really not enough money to send his kids to college and stuff like that. That's why he want me to...try and get into the service. I've always really wanted to jump out of airplanes. When I was in high school, I wanted to join the Free Fall Club, Sky Diver's Club. My parents didn't want me to, so the best thing I could think of... is to go into the Army and join the Airborne. And when I enlisted, I told them that's what I wanted to do.

One day, during boot camp, my drill instructor pulled me up and held me up on the shoulder. He says to everyone, "This is a Vietcong. You guys, when you go out there, shoot and ask questions later." I didn't think about it at that time. It didn't bother me at all at that time. It was just one of those things soldiers had to know – who they were fighting and what they looked like.

After training, the whole company was going to be rotated to Germany... and then from Germany, they would ship on to Vietnam. I said, "Well, if we're going to Vietnam anyways, why not just go over there?" I felt like I went through this training, I might as well use it. I volunteered for Vietnam. Two days later, I was shipping out. That was sometime in December of '68.

I landed at Tan Son Nhut Air Force Base. We got rushed to waiting busses and these busses just took off. I guess the place was under attack. This is the very first experience I had that I cannot forget. We rushed into these barracks, it was like a holding area before you get shipped out to a unit. About one o'clock in the morning the next day, the whole place came under attack. Some medics came into the barracks, asking everybody to volunteer some blood. Nobody would give. They started to walk back out and I said, "Hey, do I count?" The medic said, "Yeah, you do." So we went out and...we got into a tent and there was a guy lying there on a table and the medic asked me to lie down on the table for the transfusion. I was just looking at that blood going through this tube and going into the other guy's arm and I said, "This guy's really going to make it, man." Ten minutes later, the medic started taking the tube out. He said, "There's no need for you to give any-more blood. He's dead." It pissed me off. I got up and I kicked the table that this guy was lying on. I was in a rage. I wanted to turn it over and throw it out. I guess I was screaming. They said I was saying things like, "What the hell are you, prejudiced or something? You don't want my blood? Just don't die out on me." It was weird. All that time...when I was laying there, I was thinking about all the other guys who didn't want to give blood.

After about two months, we changed to G Company, 75th Ranger Battalion. Our mission was to go out where they suspect the VC (Vietcong) or North Vietnamese, record what we observe, then tell our commanders where it is on the map. Afterwards, they'll send in the grunts. The first six months, everything was great for us. About two months after that,

My generation would protest anything that our government did. I'm not saying that was wrong. Our involvement in Vietnam needed to be protested but...

everything seemed to start to fall apart. We started to suffer some causality. At Landing Zone Baldy, the VCs decided to attack that night and they overran the area. I lost one of my teammates. At that time too, that's when I got my Purple Heart. Two days later, another Purple Heart. The first evening when they came in, I shot a VC about a foot away from me. He's not the first one who I shot. You know, shooting somebody from afar is nothing. It doesn't really bother you. But shooting somebody that close hits you really hard later on. It was really dark and when the flash from the muzzle from my weapon came through, I saw his face. It was like looking at myself. I never thought of it before; it took me about 25 years for this thing to start coming back. It doesn't hit you right away.

Funny but scary moments

There were some sad moments…there were also funny moments. After our base was attacked, we went to the hospital area where a bunch of us got treated, but we had to walk back. The rest of them were already back and I was walking back wearing these cut-off shorts and my thongs. I looked just like a Vietnamese and I guess, at that time, everybody was kind of jittery because of the previous night's sneak attack. I was just walking this road, trying to go back over there and I had guns pointed at me…I was looking at them and I said, "Sgt. Odem, help!" Sgt. Odem says, "Just tell them who won the World Series, 1967." I said, "Was it the Yankees or the Dodgers?" 'Cause I didn't know, I wasn't a baseball fan anyways. And Odem says, "He's one of us. Don't shoot him."

This snake is probably one of the funniest and also the scariest at the same time…We're clearing out the whole place, starting to layout this area, and I said, "Well, I'm going to go up this hill and…go to the bathroom." So I sat by the bush, pulled my pants down and started doing my thing, and just…at the right side of my head, I saw something going…back and forth. I casually glanced over…and saw the head of this python and it's 17 feet long. It's just about a foot away, just swaying side to side. I was scared! I rolled over, had my rifle and just let out a burst, fully on automatic. I was rolling down this hill, pants down to my knees…and I can't stop. Finally, I got caught between these trees and got up. I'm running down the hill, pulling my pants up at the same time and here comes four other guys. "What is it? What is it?" I said, "Man, the scariest thing." They said, "What? A Vietcong?…North Vietnamese?…Tiger?" I said, "No, that!" And I pointed at it, 'cause that thing was coming down. They all kind of looked at the snake, and it…reared back like it's going down the hill.

Someone had enough sense to say, "Okay, aim for the head." We all aimed for the head…and let out a burst and another burst and this thing just kept coming…We all ran out of bullets and we ran down the hill…finally it stopped. Everybody was trying to tell the other, "You check it out." Finally, one of the big guys went up there…and poked it. He said, "Yeah, it's dead!"

No hero's welcome

I left in October '69. I was in a little freak accident. We had to jump out from the helicopter. There was supposed to be a hill and it was just full of elephant grasses; they grow very, very tall and very thick. I was the first one out. I jumped out…and landed on a rock, hit my right foot and fractured it. I had to stay in the hospital for a while and within that two weeks, they looked in my record and said, "Well, you know that you've only got about a month left in service. What do you want to do?" I said, "I think I want to go home." The new CO (Commanding Officer) came in and said, "I heard you're leaving. Well, I just prepared some paper work over here for an extension. I can give you another stripe…You can be an E-6, right now, just sign over here…and stay with us for a while longer." I said, "No sir. I think I have spent enough time here."

The Second World War soldiers came back and they have this welcome with open arms…parades. I guess even though you don't really look for it, you kind of wish it was the same way – not necessarily a parade or anything like that. You would like people to welcome you. Nobody really welcomed us. My generation would protest anything that our government did. I'm not saying that it was wrong. A lot of them were right. Our involvement in Vietnam needed to be protested, but…they should have been protesting the government and making the government the heavy. Instead, it was the soldiers who were coming back and they were made the heavies. As a soldier, you really don't have any choice, okay? Your job is to do what the government tells you to do. These protesters are the guys who are supposedly some of your friends, some of the guys you grow up with. These are the guy who are supposed to welcome you back, but instead, these are the guys who are calling you baby killers.

I could never really talk about Vietnam, always avoided it. My friend George, he understood. He and I never really talked about Vietnam; we never told anybody we were veterans. I really did avoid all the other veterans…so I had nobody to talk to.

Interviewed by Ken Mochizuki.

Milton WAN

Vietnam War
Army, 239th Infantry, 1967-1969
Electrician 4th Grade

I went to...a Chinese elementary school and high school in Saigon. My family is middle class family, so we are pretty well-off. We had a car and we had servants, one cooking for us, one washing laundry for us. I don't have to worry about anything. All I do is go to school and play and everything is just going well for me.

Back in 1962 or '63, you can see a lot of explosion in the theater, or...Buddhist monk demonstrations and sometimes fighting in the streets. My grandparents lived two blocks up the street from my house and sometimes I had to go to my grandparents' house to stay overnight. We walked during the night time...about two blocks and a lot of soldiers would be standing on the corner. They're guarding something. All of a sudden, it was boom-boom-boom. The people fight and then we just had to hurry up and go back to my grandparents' house.

The South Vietnamese Army

Everybody in Vietnam, when you reach the age 18, you have to apply for the identification card...but you have to go to police station to apply for the card. Once you register, you are eligible for the draft.

The Vietnamese soldier is lawless. They had gun, they had grenade and

Later, they sent a letter to my home: You are inducted to the Army. I'm kind of excited because I had seen the GI in Vietnam and I don't mind serving the U.S. Army.

then they became unreasonable and abused their authority. I don't want to get involved with that. A lot of friends of mine came back from the Vietnamese Army and told me that they are trained about two weeks and then they are sent over to the front line and fight against the V.C. (Vietcong). How much can you get from training in two weeks? What are your chances if you go out there? The V.C. are well-trained, they are under the ground. And without any skill, any training, or any expertise, you look for the V.C.? Forget it! You're dead in the water. Just dead.

When I finish my high school...my father put me in the hotel that he was managing – the Bachelor Officer Quarter and the Bachelor Enlisted Men's Quarter. I work there and I know a lot of GI. I start doing little black-market trading, exchange money. I know that if I want out of the country, I got to have some money. When I have money, I decide it's time to leave...I had to pay $1,000 – up front. And then it's no guarantee whether you reach Hong Kong or not. I was young. I didn't even think about anything. I just think about maybe I can pay the money and get me out of here.

[I escaped to Hong Kong but ran into a lot of problems trying to get an identification card that would allow me to get a passport. After a lot of confusion and hassle], I landed in Portland, Ore., and then Portland to Seattle, Wash. It feels fresh, all cold, feels good, just like...I've been in this kind of world before. I think maybe my mother gave me a lot of input about America, stories, stuff like that. It feels like home.

At the Hong Kong embassy on the way to the U.S., all immigrants have to sign the paper saying you have the right to immigrate to the country, you have the right to serve the country. You had to sign…the Draft Selective Service. Later, they sent a letter to my home: "You are inducted to the Army."

I'm not worried about it. I'm kind of excited because I had seen the GI in Vietnam and I don't mind serving the U.S. Army. Seeing American soldiers in Vietnam, I don't think about the war, I think about…some kind of security. You got paid and you got taken care of and you were in a nice uniform. In Vietnam, I compared the Vietnamese soldier and the GI; there are a lot differences. When I got my draft notice, I said, "Okay, that's fine. I'm happy to go to be United States Army." I didn't know whether they were going to send me to Vietnam or not.

Back in Vietnam

We landed in Bien Hoa, which is the processing center for all the GIs when they get to Vietnam. When I came out of the airplane, I saw all these Vietnamese soldiers. They're so small to me. Maybe when I came over to the United States, I see everything so big. When I go there, I say, "Oh my God, those guys don't have enough nutrition…They're just so skinny." I was just wondering how they can defend themselves.

I was stationed at 3rd Field Hospital as a driver for a sergeant, a lifer who wanted to make a lot of money out of Vietnam. He said, "Wan, let's do some business together. We can make some money out here." And he start talking about how he had a lot of air conditioning. He said, "You know a lot of people outside of Vietnam and you can sell it to them. I got a lot of air conditioning and a lot of bed sheets…And I got a lot of beer. I can support you 240 cases a day."

A lot of people work in the mess hall on the American compound…dump a lot of garbage, sometimes a whole can of ham unopened…People pick it up. There's a lot of stealing. They just steal food out of the compound, throw it outside and some people pick it up and sell it to market and they split the money. Both American and Vietnamese…are interested in making money…except a few because they really are fighting for the country.

Sometimes, Vietnamese civilians give me a little look, especially when I eat at a restaurant by myself and I order what they order. And then people are talking, "Hey, how come this GI knows how to eat Vietnamese food like that? He must be Vietcong." U.S. soldiers, they're still surprised too. One time, I went to pick up my sergeant at the BEQ, the Bachelor Enlisted Quarter…and I had to wait for my sergeant. There's a little bar upstairs so I went in there to…have a drink. As soon as he's done, the sergeant comes in and says, "Out!" I said, "I just want a drink." The sergeant says, "No, out, out! You're not supposed to have your weapon here." My weapon's here, but I emptied it before I come in the building. I told him, "I know it. What's wrong?" He just kept screaming at me. It's a little bit discrimination. He sees I'm Oriental. Even though I wear a U.S. uniform, he doesn't give a shit. Luckily, it's in the city, it's not that bad. Like in the countryside, when the fight erupts and your fellow Americans don't know what's going on. They see an Oriental and they just shoot. They don't know what side you're on.

They tried to recruit me to stay another year…They said, "When you re-enlist, we'll give you $5,000 and you can stay in Vietnam for another year." I said no. It's kind of dangerous in Vietnam. I didn't know how dangerous it was. I wanted to come back to the United States. I didn't want to get killed in Vietnam.

Interviewed by Ken Mochizuki and David Elliott.

Harvey WATANABE

World War II and Korean War
Military Intelligence Service, Allied Translator & Interpreter Section,
1941-1945
1st Calvary Division, 1951-1952
1st Lieutenant

In the late summer of 1940, they started registering for the draft. I went to the local draft office. At that time, we were working in Delano, Calif. My registration number was 15. And then in November, in Washington, D.C., they had a drawing of the registration numbers to see who would be drafted first in each district. I was listening to the radio and the seventh one they pulled out of the fishbowl was number 15. The entire community gave me a great big party there at Christmas time.

When they started the draft, so many volunteers came in right off the bat, I didn't have to report until February of '41. They gave me my uniform and put me on a train and sent me to Fort Lewis, Wash. I never took the basic training. I went straight into the Army.

July 1941, when we were in maneuvers in California, I was called to the company commander's tent. I went there and a captain came out and handed me a Japanese book, an elementary school reader. He says, "Can you read this?" And I read it. And he says, "What does it say?" and I told him. That's all. He never said another word. That's when I think he was going around,

They had a drawing of the registration numbers to see who would be drafted first in each district. The seventh one they pulled out of the fishbowl was my number, 15.

marking the Nisei [second generation Japanese Americans] that he wanted.

On Dec. 7, 1941, my bunk mate was waking me up, "Get up...The radio's on. You've got to listen to it!" I listened to the radio: Pearl Harbor was bombed! We took off about mid-afternoon and drove from Fort Lewis through...Highway 99 and drove right in front of Boeing and saw all the camouflage on the building. Our outfits wound up in Burlington, Wash., and continued on Deception Pass Bridge. Deception Pass Bridge is actually two separate bridges. It's a bridge that goes from the mainland to a small island in the middle of the pass and from there, another bridge finishes off and hooks up to Whidbey Island. We set up our two guns on that bridge, on that island and we had that set up by the late night of Dec. 7.

The end of January...they moved a bunch of us to the Olympic Peninsula. Our job was to...drive Highway 101 and just keep a lookout on things. I did that for maybe about a week then word came: "You turn in your gun. We're going to take you back to Fort Lewis." Well, what's going on? In the meantime, before I left Burlington, a lot of the Nisei guys I ran across were no longer doing anything. Their commander had taken them off anything they thought was sensitive. I knew that something was going on regarding us. And they drove me back to Fort Lewis and – lo and behold – there were about 250 other Niseis, all GIs. All we're doing is sleeping and eating and gambling and wondering what's going to happen. Eventually, there were about 350 of us. In March 1942, we soldiers were "evacuated" from the West Coast.

Military Intelligence

From 1942 to 1945, Nisei soldiers who knew Japanese were sent to language school training in Minnesota and assigned to the Military Intelligence Service (MIS). Our school hours were eight in the morning to nine in the night, with no study periods. We had to study after nine o' clock. Lights out was at 10 so a lot of guys were just studying in the latrines because there weren't any other lights on.

I was later assigned to Australia where, I had a small team…and we took care of all technical documents concerning aircraft, all mechanical, all tanks and things of that nature. We would translate them. They gave me the job of screening all of those captured documents that came in. For over a year, I was opening crates and going through them and taking parts to the screening board, suggesting what we should do with it. The name was Allied Translator and Interpreter Service (ATIS)…which had New Zealanders, Australians, Chinese, Greeks, American Navy, and, of course, the U.S. But the main work was being done by Nisei.

When we got to Manila…I was driving a staff car…taking different officers to different places. I left off a couple of colonels at headquarters and I got back into the staff car to leave. A Filipino guy reaches in from the window and grabs the steering wheel. In his left hand, he has a big bolo knife. I thought he figured he caught a Japanese soldier making an escape. I started talking to him in English. I wasn't being hard on him. I was just asking him: "Did you mistake me for being a Japanese?" He understood English pretty good. He let go of the steering wheel a couple of minutes…later, then he said, "Bye, bye."

From one war to another

After working in occupied Japan, I came back to Minneapolis January 1946. That's where my wife was living. I went to Minneapolis School of Business and I worked for a laundry for a year. We moved to Seattle in the summer of '48.

I was obligated to serve in the military for five years and it was four years and 11 months when they gave me notice saying, "Report to Korea." Telephone call, three o'clock in the morning. If you have three or more children, you can ignore the call. We only had two.

When we pulled out of Korea and I was in Japan, I got a phone call saying, "Guess who this is? It's your brother, Jack. I'm calling from Zamma and I am supposed to go to Korea tomorrow." I went to Zamma and pulled him out of the infantry replacement line. He just about went bonkers. I told him, "Look, I've just finished six years of wartime duty and your brother got two purple hearts in Europe. Korea's the worst place in the world for infantrymen. I don't want you going there, that's why I'm doing this." Three years later when we got together, he said, "Harvey, I want to apologize to you for getting so mad at you. That's the best thing that ever happened to me."

When you leave military intelligence, they tell you, "Don't talk." There were times I wanted to talk about my war experiences. I remember one time in a restaurant in Burien, Wash., the restaurant went dead silent because I got so teed off at a guy for talking against Japanese American veterans that I told him off. This was probably 15 years ago. He was saying, "You guys couldn't have been doing things like that. Things didn't happen like that." I just said, "You're the liar, not me." I said it in such a loud voice that everybody went quiet. People don't know the extent to which the Nisei MIS served. Australia, New Guinea, Philippines, Pacific islands, China – you name them, the Nisei MIS were there.

Interviewed by Ken Mochizuki and Pei Pei Sung.

Harvey Hideo Watanabe (left) with brother Tom Toru Watanabe, 1946
–Courtesy of Harvey Hideo Watanabe.

Larry WONG

Vietnam War
Marine Corps, 1st Marine Air Wing, 1961-1969
Corporal

I was a little bit restless at school…so I just joined. I wasn't drafted. A couple of my friends from high school were joining the Marine Corps. I thought, if I went to someplace, I want to be well trained enough to be able to survive what I was going to go through. And I was of the understanding that the Marine Corps took care of their own. At that time, we were right in the middle of the war; it was very heated, so there wasn't much question…that I would be going to Vietnam.

I went into basic training October of '66. Afterwards, I went in about eight or nine months of electronics training, at radio repair. I was transferred to Vietnam in February of '68.

Landing in Da Nang Airport, I saw a lot of explosions going around the perimeters of the base. Plane landed, we got off, got into some shelter, and some of the guys got on the plane. It's funny, 'cause as I was getting off the plane, another soldier was just pointing at me. "You're my replacement. Good luck, sucker!" That was my initiation to my in country. Back in the states, they needed two people to go to Vietnam and everybody else in the shop was married except for another guy and myself. So we looked at each other and said, "Okay, we will go, 'cause we don't have any attachments." I was thinking…when I was on the plane landing…maybe I shouldn't have said that. Should've just kept my mouth shut, never volunteered.

As I was getting off the plane in Vietnam, another soldier was just pointing at me. 'You're my replacement. Good luck, sucker!' That was my initiation.

Small acts of rebellion

I got off the plane, took my orders to the headquarters' office and I was surprised to find they didn't expect me there. I could've never shown up and, frankly, it wouldn't have made any difference. I remember it was muddy, that red…clay type like in Hawaii. Showed up at the office and they asked me if I could type. I made the mistake of letting them know I could type. I ended up typing reports. That's when I sensed that something was wrong, something was amiss. I just didn't feel like it was right, what was happening, based on the information I had there. A lot of it I've blocked out because it was a distasteful experience. That's when I began to sense — I guess I'd call it my rebellion. After the first few days, I constantly asked to get out of the office, go to the tech shop and just be a technician. Eventually I got there, and then I didn't like that so I ended up…volunteering to build sandbags and build bunkers around the tech shop. It was either…be with a person of a mentality that I didn't agree with, or be by myself where I would just do the job and be left alone. That was much better. That was my option at the time.

When we went out on our patrol outside the perimeter area, I remember looking at a hooch and seeing a pot of hot rice and some veggies cooking. The older people there tend to wear black…pajama-type clothes. And I remember my Grandma Wong always used to wear black pajama-type clothes — even a black apron. It reminded me of the farm at Yakima. Just the essence reminded me of Grandma cooking at the kitchen in Yakima.

I never became close to anybody and, frankly, I don't think I became that close with people who were Marines. You close your emotions and don't become friendly with people because it's dangerous; it can cost you your life. During training, the process was to brainwash you, and make your mind set so that you didn't think about other people as human. It's a dehumanizing factor and consequently you use the term "gook" rather than saying he's Vietnamese, which implies that he is a human.

In September of '69, I got back. I came home for a 30-days leave...I remember coming on base and...we stood in inspection. They pulled the uniform out of my suit bag and it was wrinkled. I didn't think about it at the time...I realize now that there was a change in my mindset as regards to being in the service. I could not openly fight it without being dishonorably discharged. I figure it would screw me up...so I guess...I didn't go along with the program. I could've shined my brass and polished my boots, but didn't. I was ready to get out. After I came back from Vietnam, I was ready to get out of the Marine Corps.

I think part of the reason was that my experiences of war had a very negative effect. I experienced death, destruction and that isn't good for anybody...War has a negative impact on the planet...and even those who are not associated with it – parents, families – had to go through a lot of stress, seeing it on TV everyday. It's not a good thing at all. They say that war is a way to boost the economy. I think it's a negative way to boost the economy. It's all and all just bad business and it's unprofitable. Maybe it's profitable for a short-term period, selling the machinery, all the things that take to run a war, but in the long run...you see the negative impact today.

Adjusting to civilian life

I was happy to be back. I was happy to have clean, ceramic facilities to go to the bathroom. Clean places to be. Air was clean, and the idea that I didn't have to worry about...jumping out of the bunk and heading for the bunker, getting blown up.

I went back to work at Boeing. I lasted to the first of January. It was a big factory and I couldn't stand it. After Boeing, I went to work as a waiter. After several jobs, for some reason at that time [1980s], bottom seemed to fall out for me. What I'm told now is that it was a lot of suppressed grief, a lot of suppressed stress that finally came through. It's like a pressure cooker...and finally, there's enough pressure and the top comes off. So now, I'm starting to get a handle on it.

I still perceive within the government...that animalistic nature within ourselves to glorify death in the name of some cause, or destruction in the name of some cause. That's a vain glory, I think. I went to a lot of war movies when I was growing up. What I saw with John Wayne and the various other war movies, I grew up being influenced by that and back then, I saw honor. I think it's important at this time, in our space on the planet that we really strive for peace, that we really sincerely strive for peace.

Interviewed by Ken Mochizuki.

David "Gobby" WOO (1912-1992)

World War II
Army Air Corps, 1942-1945
Sergeant

I went into the curio business, Chinese arts. I did that for a while. I had a shop, but that didn't work out because I couldn't get any stuff from China because the war was on. So I closed it up and joined the Army. I volunteered. I said, "What the hell. They'll get me sooner or later so I might as well go." So I went. Most of the guys were going in anyway.

I thought I would make it easy on myself and volunteered for the Coast Guard and I thought I was going to stay in the states. They took me in and they asked me what tribe I belonged to. I said, "I don't belong to any tribe. I'm Chinese." They said, "Oh, we can't take you… because we have to have an affidavit from certain respectable people saying that you're a person of good respect and dependable and all of that." So I went out and got the head of immigration, who was my father's friend, and he wrote out that I'm from a good family and all that. I went to another guy, a White guy – it all has to be White guys – I got three references and by then, they accepted me. I was in the Army Air Corps.

I had been thinking about it…either I get killed or I get taken prisoner of war. Here, I'm a prisoner of war; I guess I'm lucky.

I graduated from aerial gunnery school and they assigned me to a squadron. One pilot grabbed me off right away and said, "Hey, I know I want you up in my crew. We might land up in China and I want somebody to speak Chinese." Instead of going to China, I went to England. I made six missions, and boom – went down. I was involved in the first mission over German proper…

over Dunkirk, where we were looking for a Japanese ship that we were going to bomb. We hit it and on the way out, they hit us. I had a piece of flak in my foot… and a lot of muscle sprains. I couldn't get up and there was an army surrounding me anyway…So they grabbed me and they put me on a horse-drawn wagon, paraded me through the main part of town.

They gave me a little first aid…and after interviewing me, they sent me off to interrogation camp…Dulag Luft. There, I was locked up for over a week. A little dungeon. There was no air or nothing and they wouldn't let me out unless I talked. They asked me where I was from and what race I was, what nationality I was and I just gave them the answer: "I'm American." And I kept saying that and they said, "You're not American. You're something else." They slapped me. They kept asking and asking then they gave up and let me out in the middle of the yard where other prisoners were. This was Stalag 17. When we got chased out of there because the Russians were coming, we had over 4,500 – all Americans. There were others, but I don't know how many. There were Russians. There were French, English.

I was in four or five different camps. I was in Cell 8B in one camp where the Indians were. And they grabbed me right away and said, "Hey, you're our brother." I said, "I'm not your brother." There was another compound there where they locked up the Russians. They had people who looked like Chinese yelling at me. They were Mongolians. And this one GI came along and said, "They want you to give them something to eat." I said, "How about giving me something to eat?"

I was in prisoner-of-war (POW) camps all together about 27 months. I was in what they called the white house… which was where the people who have something to do with the running of the camp stayed. I was in charge of the mail...see that it's rightly distributed and copies sent out and stamped and all that. Also I was co-editor of the underground news. One guy who speaks German...and I got together every day and wrote up the news sheet. As soon as the Germans are gone and the lights are out, we get somebody to go around and read the news stories off. We would make up most of it – morale builders. We wrote about how many kilometers we advanced, how our troops are going to come forward and how everything is good, nothing is bad. We get the German newspapers and he reads them. Some of it's pretty bad. Like the Battle of the Bulge, we never mentioned that. We build the guys up. A lot of guys went sick, crazy.

I wasn't a bit afraid of anything. I took everything in because I knew I was in for the long wait. I had been thinking about it...either I get killed or I get taken prisoner of war. Here, I'm a prisoner of war; I guess I'm lucky.

Well, on that forced march, we were walking one night, we heard a lot of gunfire. The Americans had contacted the Germans. It took approximately two or three weeks before the Americans...caught up with us. Finally...an American captain came in and said, "Gentlemen, you are free." Now when the captain came to tell us we're free, everybody cried. When I saw that, there wasn't a guy who didn't cry.

We waited for over a month for transportation. Gen. Dwight Eisenhower came... and said, "Gentlemen, I know you waited a long time. I can get you transportation on the ship – very crowded conditions – and send you home right now." And we all yelled, "Send us home right now!" So they did. They put us in the hold where ...we slept four stacks high and each guy got eight hours. That's all. Eight hours up, some guy would come and kick me and say, "Get out of here. It's my turn." As soon as they take over the bunk, I go to the soup line. I sit there all day long. As soon as I finish it, I go right back to the end of the line and start eating again. I was hungry.

When they said, "We see land," I got up there on deck and I looked and looked and looked at the Statue of Liberty. That made me real happy.

"Gobby" Woo, founding member (far right), pictured far right with fellow World War II veterans and members of the American Legion Cathay Post #186, 1946.
—Courtesy of American Legion Cathay Post #186 Seattle, Wash.

I really thought, when I get back...I'm going to the gambling house and I'm going to gamble one $1,000-hand with my back pay. I'm going to double my money right there. And the second thing I'll do, I'll organize a veterans' group because I know all of my friends were in the service. So I did both of them.

We used to help each other whenever we needed help. A lot of these guys who went in first to the military were China-borns. They don't speak any English hardly and they need help in filing for this and that. So the ones who spoke English, we ran the organization. And then all these guys from China who didn't speak English come in and ask for aid. We welcome them and do what we can. We weren't working anyways. They had a lot of difficulty because they couldn't get wives from overseas because, in the old days, you can't unless you're a citizen. We asked a lot of them to file for citizenship. They get to be a citizen after being in the service. We helped them with that and we went and filed papers for them down in Immigration and Naturalization Service. And they went to China and they got married over there then came back.

At first we met at Twin Dragons Café, that's an old restaurant [in Seattle's International District]. Then...some of the next meetings we had at Chong Wa. And then we rented quarters on Eighth Avenue where the *Chinese Post* is now. We stayed there quite a while. And we did a little gambling there, taking a little kitty and the police tolerated us. They closed up the whole Chinatown, but they didn't close us up. Then the Chinese Baptist Church was for sale and everybody was real tired of drinking and everybody was getting old, so some guys said, "Let's buy the building and see what we can do." We bought that and sold it for a real good profit. We're living off the profits right now. We use quite a few thousand a year for the scholarships for young Chinese Americans and we donate to a lot of causes. We don't keep anything at all.

Interviewed by Ron Chew.

Highlights from the History of
Asian Pacific Americans in the U.S. Armed Forces

1814 During the War of 1812, Filipinos fight with American forces to defeat the British in the decisive Battle of New Orleans.

1862 Six Chinese Americans documented as serving in the U.S. Civil War.

1898 Eight Asian Pacific Americans are among the Navy sailors killed when the *USS Maine* explodes while docked at Havana, Cuba. The sinking of the American battleship starts the Spanish-American War.

1899 – 1901 U.S. establishes military rule over the Philippines instead of granting independence after the Spanish-American War. Filipinos rebel in what Western historians refer to as the Philippine Insurrection. The U.S. Army forms the 1st Company of Macabebe Scouts with Filipino civilians to fight the rebels.

1901 U.S. President William McKinley signs General Order No. 40, permitting the U.S. Navy to recruit up to 500 Filipinos from the Philippine Islands to enlist in the Naval Insular Force in the Philippines.

1913 Congressional Medal of Honor is awarded to the first soldier of Asian/Pacific Islander descent, Pvt. Jose B. Nisperos of the 34th Company of Philippine Scouts.

1915 Congressional Medal of Honor is awarded to Fireman 2nd Class Telesforo Trinidad.

1917 – 1918 Asian Pacific Americans are members of the U.S. forces during World War I.

1918 WWI veterans of Asian Pacific ancestry are given right to naturalization.

1925 U.S. Supreme Court decides in *Toyota vs. U.S.,* that Issei [first generation Japanese American] war veterans are ineligible for naturalization.

1935 Nye-Lea Bill grants naturalization rights to 500 World War I veterans of Asian decent.

1940 U.S. Alien Registration Act of 1940 classifies Korean immigrants as subjects of Japan and thus "enemy aliens."

1941 Dec. 7 Pearl Harbor Naval Base is attacked by Japanese bombers, launching the United States into World War II. Two thousand Nisei [second generation Japanese American] soldiers help defend against enemy attack.

1941 Dec. 20 Congress passes a resolution allowing "virtually unlimited enlistment and employment of the Pilipino-Americans in the war effort."

1942 Jan. 19 All soldiers of Japanese ancestry in the U.S. Army classified as 4C enemy alien.

1942 Feb. 19 Secretary of War Henry L. Stimson announces formation of the 1st Filipino Infantry Regiment. President Franklin Roosevelt signs Executive Order 9066, begins the internment of Americans of Japanese decent to concentration camps scattered throughout the Midwest.

1942 Congressional Medal of Honor is awarded to Sgt. Jose Cabalfin Calugas, Sr.

1943 U.S. Army calls for 1,500 Nisei volunteers; 9,507 second-generation Japanese Americans respond. They are assigned to the all-Nisei 100th Battalion and 442nd Regimental Combat Team (RCT).

1943 U.S. issues order exempting Koreans from "enemy alien" status due largely to protesting from communities of Korean decent.

1944 The all-Chinese American 14th Air Service Group serves in Asia and provides critical ground support for the Flying Tigers. The 1st and 2nd Filipino Infantry Regiments secretly arrive on the Japanese-held Philippine Islands to pave the way for Gen Douglas MacArthur's return. The 100th Battalion/442nd RCT battle through Italy and rescue the "Lost Battalion" in France. Japanese Americans of the Military Intelligence Service provide essential information that leads to American victories in the Pacific.

1945 April The 100th Battalion/442nd RCT overrun the Gothic Line, the German stronghold in Italy. The victory breaks the German defenses and turns the tide of the war. Congressional Medal of Honor is awarded to PFC Sadao Munemori.

1946 U.S. President Harry Truman presents the 7th Presidential Unit Citation to the 100th Battalion and 442nd RCT.

1947 Military Base Agreement between United States and Republic of the Philippines allows U.S. Navy to be the only military branch and foreign country to have the right to enlist citizens of the Philippines into the U.S. Armed Forces.

1947 U.S. President Harry Truman bans segregation within the U.S. Armed Forces.

1950 North Korean troops advance past the 38th Parallel dividing North and South Korea. World War II Asian Pacific American veterans return to duty. More Asian Pacific Americans volunteer or are drafted and serve in every branch of the military.

1951 Congressional Medals of Honor are awarded to Cpl. Hiroshi "Hershey" Miyamura, Sgt. Leroy A. Mendonca and PFC Herbert K. Pililaau.

Mid 1950s United States sends military advisors to assist the South Vietnamese Army in its armed conflict with troops from North Vietnam and Vietcong guerrillas. U.S. military troops begin arriving in 1960. During the course of the Vietnam War, 88,118 Asian Pacific Americans serve in all branches of the military.

1955 United States engages in a "secret war" against communist forces in Laos. U.S. CIA and military advisors recruit, train and supply members of Southeast Asian indigenous tribes to aid in their fight against Communist-backed North Vietnam. Later, those who prove they worked for the CIA are given priority as refugees to the United States.

1969 Congressional Medals of Honor are awarded to Sgt. 1st Class Rodney J.T. Yano and Cpl. Terry Teruo Kawamura.

1971 U.S. Navy formally lifts restriction once limiting Filipinos from the Philippines to the steward rating.

1972 Freedom of Information Act gives former Military Intelligence Service Nisei veterans the liberty to speak of their World War II service duties.

1983 Oct. 25-27 U.S. troops fight Cuban forces and evacuate Americans from the Caribbean island of Grenada. Japanese American Mark Yamane is among the 18 U.S. soldiers killed in action.

1991 Feb. 24 The Allies launch a ground assault to liberate Kuwait, after Iraqi President Saddam Hussein invades and annexes this neighboring country. Asian Pacific Americans are among the ground troops and naval ships.

1988 Dec. 28 U.S. President William Clinton orders air strikes against Iraq.

1999 March 24 The U.S. joins NATO's efforts to force Yugoslavian President Slobodan Milosevic to a peacekeeping agreement in Kosovo. NATO begins bombing in Yugoslavia. Asian Pacific Americans participate in bombing and peacekeeping efforts.

—Photo by Dean Wong

Index of Veterans by War

Funding for this publication is made possible by:

Prime Sponsor:

City of Seattle Department of Neighborhoods

Major Sponsor:

Rockefeller Foundation

Sponsors:

Hugh and Jane Ferguson Foundation

King County Landmarks and Heritage Commission –
    Hotel and Motel Tax Revenues

Ruth Mott Fund

PONCHO

Seattle Arts Commission

Washington Commission for the Humanities

Acknowledgements

We thank the following for their talent and dedication:

Project Coordinator
Pei Pei Sung

Community Advisory Committee
Dorothy Cordova
David Della
Mike Higashi
Joseph Kamikawa
Raymond Lew
Debbie Kashino McQuilken
Khanh Nguyen
Craig Shimabukuro
Jose Velasquez

Organizational support provided by
American Legion Cathay Post #186
The Bataan Corregidor Survivors
    Association and Their Families
Densho Project
Filipino American National
    Historical Society
Nisei Veterans Committee
Seattle Sansei

Project Interviewers
Linda Megumi Ando
Paula Bock
Ron Chew
Bianca Chinn
Cassie Chinn
Carina A. del Rosario
Ferdinand de Leon
Eydie Detera
David Elliott
Lily Eng
Heather Goheen
Seiji Hata
Cynthia Mejia-Guidici
Mei Mei Kam
Beverly Kashino
Melissa Lin
Tammy Lu
Tina Lu
Debbie Kashino McQuilken
Charlene Mano
Craig Matsuda
Ken Mochizuki
Patricia Norikane
Chanh Norsouvanh
John D. Pai
Michael Park
Vena Foster Rainwater
Pei Pei Sung
Sarah M. Vacatio
Jose Velasquez
Geneva T. Witzleben

Special thanks to the veterans who generously shared their stories
Fred Abe
Lorea T. (Patricia) Acuszaar
Luis Reyes Acuzaar
Antonio Aguon
Mariano Angeles
Warren Chan
Ark G. Chin
Henry Yun Chin
William Chin
Yao Chin
Ron Chinn
Teresita Iriarte Coalson
Gene del Rosario
Eddie N. Detera
Paul Hosoda
Mike Higashi
Joseph Kamikawa
Jimmie Kanaya
Shiro Kashino
Richard Lew Kay
Howard P. Kim
Spady Koyama
Bill Kunitsugu
Bert C. Letrondo, Sr.
Raymond Lew
James Locke
Horace Loo
Wing Chong Luke
Douglas Luna
Rosendo Luna, Sr.
Dan Mar
Frank Matsuda
Tatsuo N. Matsuda

Kim Muromoto
Mike Muromoto
Richard H. Naito
Bill Nishimura
Mack Nogaki
Katashi Oita
JoAnn L. Oligario
Kaun Onodera
Victorino Ovena
Lorenzo Umel Pimentel
Hilarion D. Polintan
Camilo M. Ramirez
Robert Satoshi Sato
Martin J. Sibonga, Sr.
Lorenzo W. Silvestre
Pete Sua
Shokichi Tokita
Jimmie A. Toy
Fe Trias
Stan Tsujikawa
Jose Velasquez
Milton Wan
Harvey Watanabe
Lawrence Wong
David Woo
Mark O. Yamane

Additional Contributors:
Lily Lee Adams
Susan Almachar
Melanie Apostel
Pacita Bunag
Cathy Chang
Heather Cameron

Pricilla del Rosario
Cabot J. Guidry
Meredith Higashi
Laurie Imamoto
Cynthia Imanaka
Charles Johnstone
Karen Johnstone
Louise Kashino
Ron King
Rekha Kuver
Amy Look
Alexis Landry
Mildred Loo
Salvacion Luna
Matthew Maeda
Sylvia Nogaki
Sumi Onodera
Pimentel Family
Jennie Pu
Kendrick Redira
Stacy Roh
Jeni Seko
Roger Serra
Linda Sim
Ja-Eun Shin
Alana Sengsi
Allice Sung
Beth Takekawa
Frank Tsuboi
Joanna Unze
Ruth Vincent
Kristi Woo
Leana Woo
Perry Woo
Yamane Family
Wing Luke Asian Museum Board
    and Staff

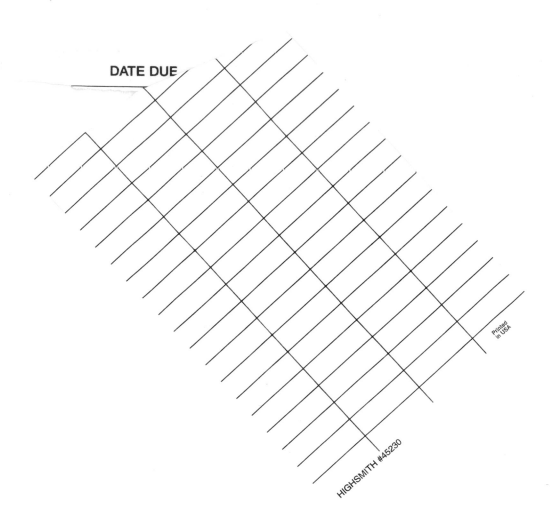

DATE DUE

HIGHSMITH #45230

Printed
in USA